LEARNING
STRUCTURES

The mission of **aha!** Process, Inc. is to positively impact the education of individuals in poverty around the world.

Payne, Ruby K., Ph.D.
   Learning Structures. Third revised edition, 2005; 141 pp.
   Bibliography pp. 140-141
   ISBN 1-929229-41-0

Ruby K. Payne, Ph.D.

Learning
Structures

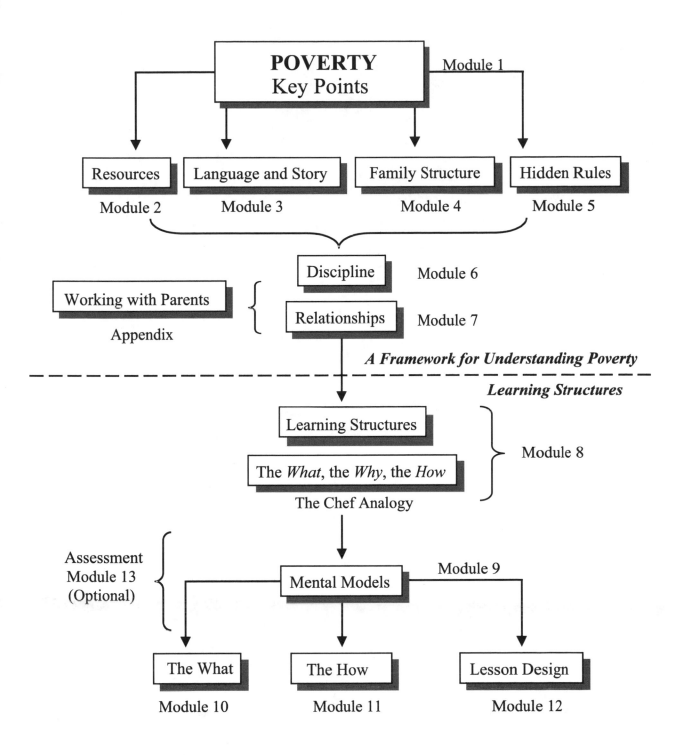

POVERTY
Key Points — Module 1

Resources — Module 2

Language and Story — Module 3

Family Structure — Module 4

Hidden Rules — Module 5

Discipline — Module 6

Relationships — Module 7

Working with Parents — Appendix

A Framework for Understanding Poverty

Learning Structures

Learning Structures

The *What*, the *Why*, the *How* — Module 8

The Chef Analogy

Assessment Module 13 (Optional)

Mental Models — Module 9

The What — Module 10

The How — Module 11

Lesson Design — Module 12

Contents

MODULE 8

LEARNING STRUCTURES: THE *WHAT*, THE *WHY*, THE *HOW*

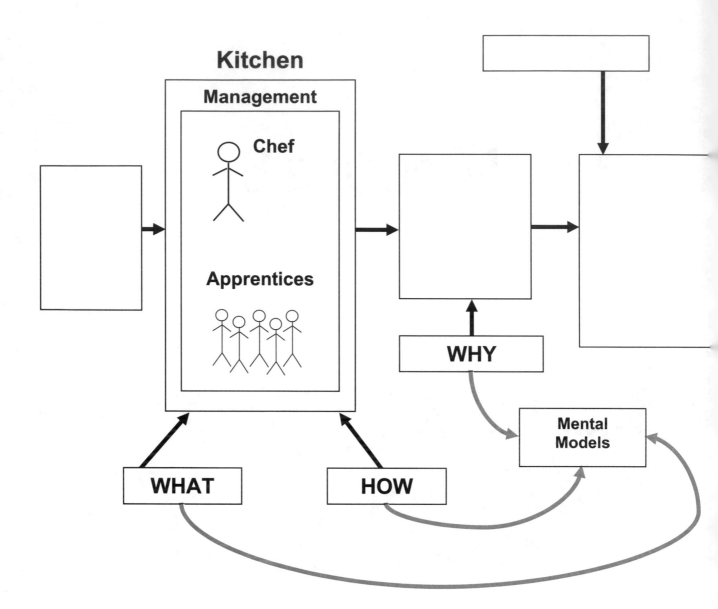

Kitchen

Management

Chef

Apprentices

WHY

Mental Models

WHAT

HOW

Full diagram in Appendix A, page 84

Processing

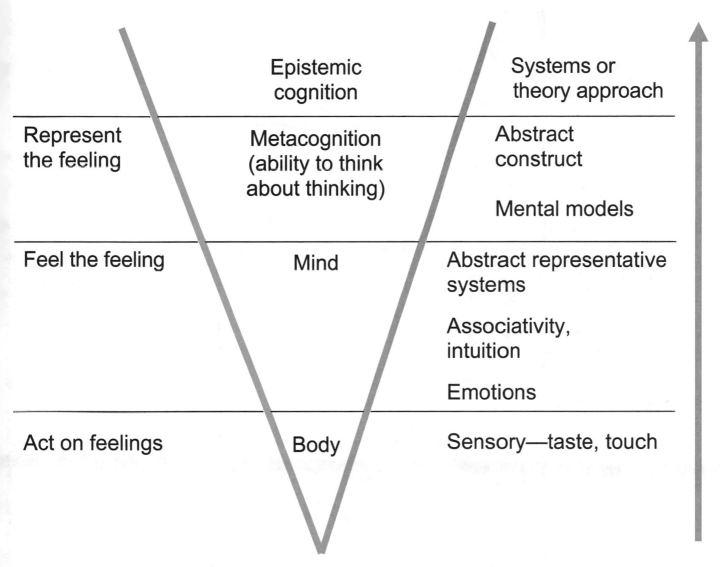

	Epistemic cognition	Systems or theory approach
Represent the feeling	Metacognition (ability to think about thinking)	Abstract construct Mental models
Feel the feeling	Mind	Abstract representative systems Associativity, intuition Emotions
Act on feelings	Body	Sensory—taste, touch

Payne Lesson Design

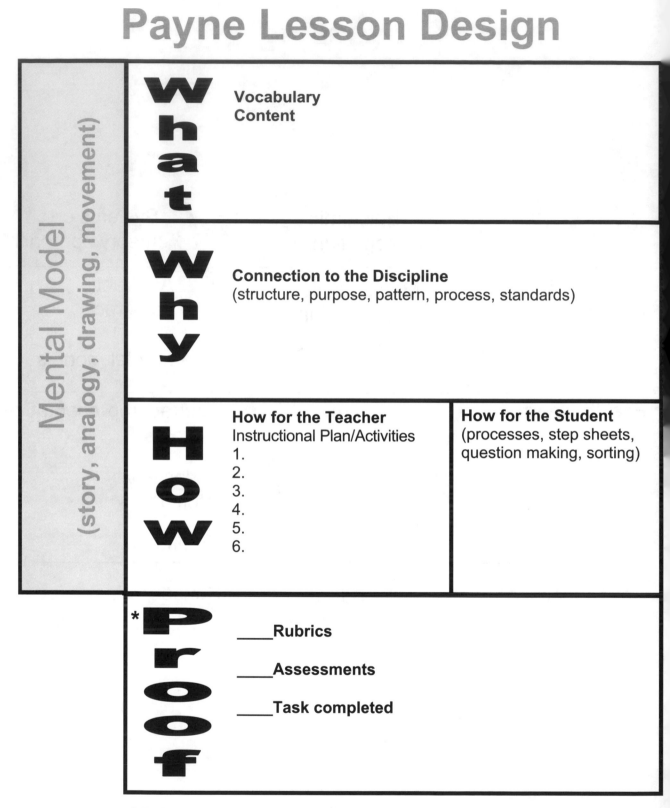

Mental Model
(story, analogy, drawing, movement)

What

Vocabulary
Content

Why

Connection to the Discipline
(structure, purpose, pattern, process, standards)

How

How for the Teacher
Instructional Plan/Activities
1.
2.
3.
4.
5.
6.

How for the Student
(processes, step sheets, question making, sorting)

*Proof

____Rubrics

____Assessments

____Task completed

* This should be shared with students.

MODULE 9

MENTAL MODELS:
HELP UNDERSTAND THE *WHY*
AND TRANSLATE THE CONCRETE
TO THE ABSTRACT

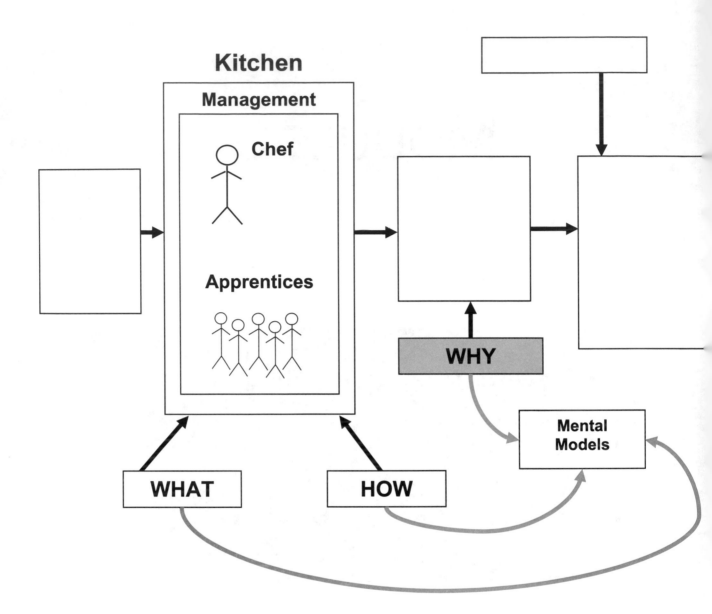

Kitchen

Management

Chef

Apprentices

WHAT

HOW

WHY

Mental Models

Full diagram in Appendix A, page 84

www.ahaprocess.com

Mental Models

To translate the concrete to the abstract, the mind needs to hold the information in a mental model. A mental model can be a two-dimensional visual representation, a story, a metaphor, or an analogy.

To understand any discipline or field of study, one must understand the mental models that the discipline uses. All disciplines are based on mental models. For example, when an individual builds a house, many discussions and words (the abstract) are used to convey what the finished house (the concrete) will be. But between the words and the finished house are blueprints. Blueprints are the translators. Between the three-dimensional concrete house and the abstract words, a two-dimensional visual translates.

When mental models are directly taught, abstract information can be learned much more quickly because the mind has a way to contain it or hold it.

One of the most important mental models for students to have is a mental model for time that includes a past, present, and future. A mental model for time is critical to understanding cause, effect, consequence, and sequence. Without a model for time, an individual cannot plan. (Please note that there are cultural differences in mental models for time; however, all cultural mental models for time do have a way to address past, present, and future.)

To access a student's mental model, use sketching or ask for a story, analogy, or metaphor.

Sketching is a particularly useful tool in better understanding what a student has stored in terms of mental models. To do sketching with students, have them draw a two-dimensional visual of how they think about a word, an idea, a person, etc.

Mental Models

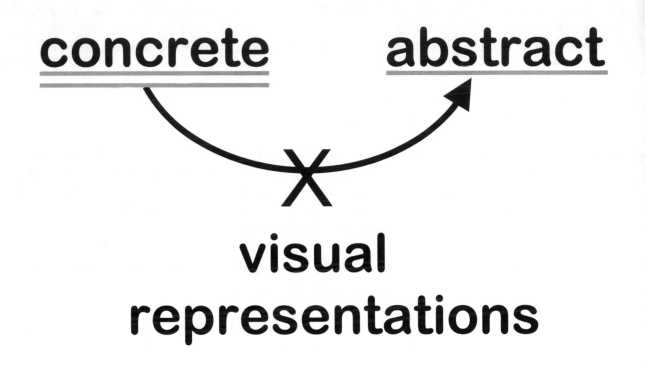

concrete   abstract

visual representations

Five Generic Mental Models for Dealing with School and Work

Space	Provides organization Helps with math and maps
Formal register	Language of money Shared understanding
Part to whole	Allows for task completion
Time	Controls impulsivity Is about planning
Decoding	Can read the language and abstract symbols

Sketching Vocabulary

Name: _____

Word	Picture

☐ WHAT ☑ WHY ☐ HOW

www.ahaprocess.com

Examples of Sketching

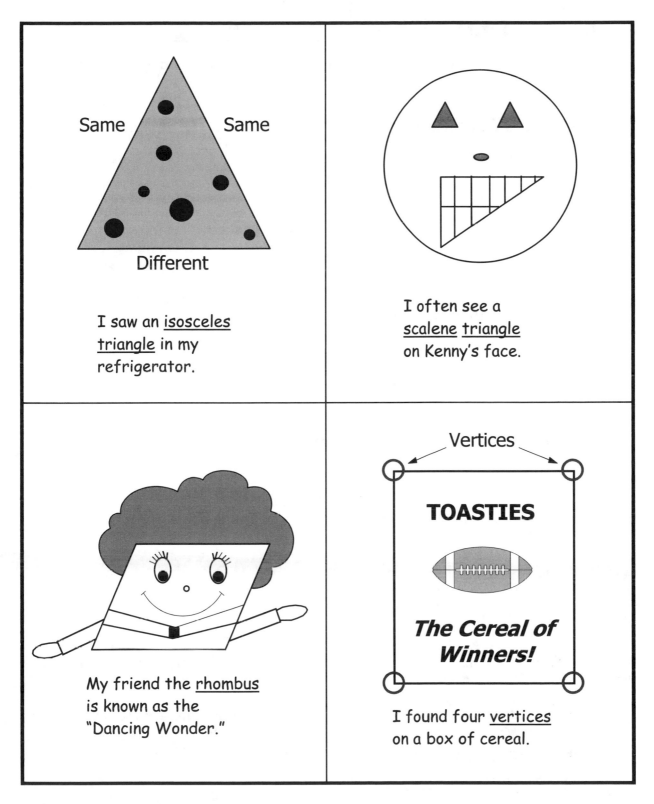

Same   Same

Different

I saw an <u>isosceles</u> <u>triangle</u> in my refrigerator.

I often see a <u>scalene</u> <u>triangle</u> on Kenny's face.

My friend the <u>rhombus</u> is known as the "Dancing Wonder."

Vertices

TOASTIES

The Cereal of Winners!

I found four <u>vertices</u> on a box of cereal.

Adapted from materials by Cathy Fields

☐ WHAT ☑ WHY ☐ HOW

Mental Model for Formal Register—Written Expression

Sentence Frame

Reminds me that each sentence must contain a capital letter and some kind of punctuation mark.

Bare-Bones Sentence

A sentence must contain a subject and an action.

The subject names a <u>person</u>, <u>place</u>, <u>thing</u>, or <u>idea</u>.

The action of the subject expresses <u>physical</u> or <u>mental</u> action.

| moved | kicked | thought | imagined |

Predicate Expanders

The predicate can be expanded by expressing the

how   when   where   why   **of the action.**

Example: The <u>waves</u> pounded relentlessly against the small sailboat

how   where

why   when

because of the violent winds during the storm.

Where	=	prepositional phrases	to, from, against, behind
How	=	adverbs	-ly ending, like or as, with/without
When	=	time	before, during, after, when, while, since
Why	=	reason	because, to, so, for

(The opening sentence of each new paragraph should contain four expanders.)

Words that describe physical characteristics, personality, numbers, and ownership.

Subject Describer

☐ WHAT ☑ WHY ☐ HOW

Source: Project Read, www.projectread.com, (800) 450-0343, Authors Victoria E. Green, Mary Lee Enfield, Ph.D.

Mental Model for Space

On which side of the tip of the arrow is the dot?

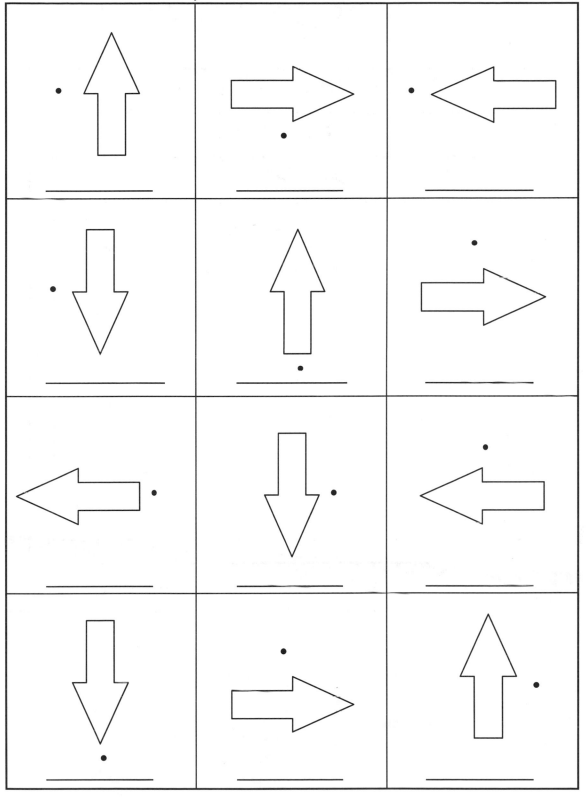

Mental Model for Social Studies

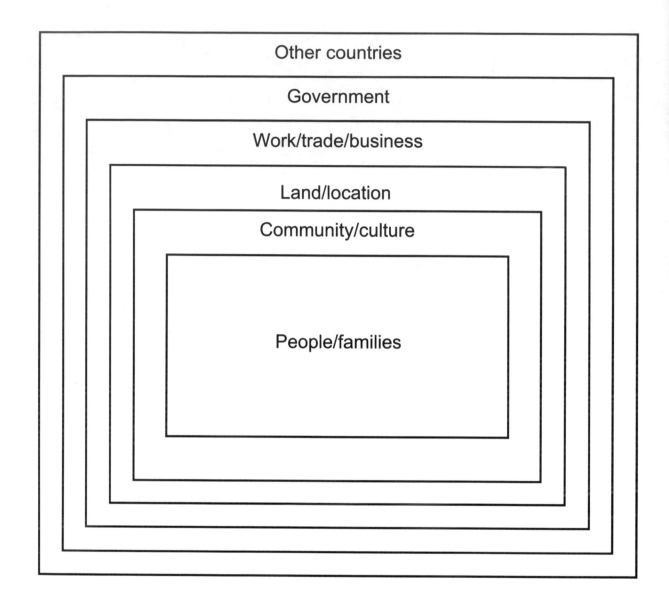

Other countries

Government

Work/trade/business

Land/location

Community/culture

People/families

☐ WHAT ☑ WHY ☐ HOW

www.ahaprocess.com

Mental Model for Social Studies

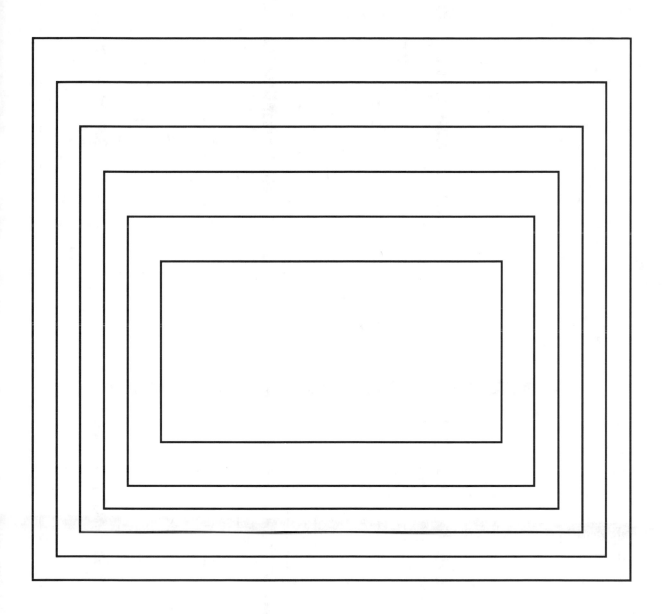

WHAT ☐ WHY ☑ HOW ☐

Mental Model for Part to Whole

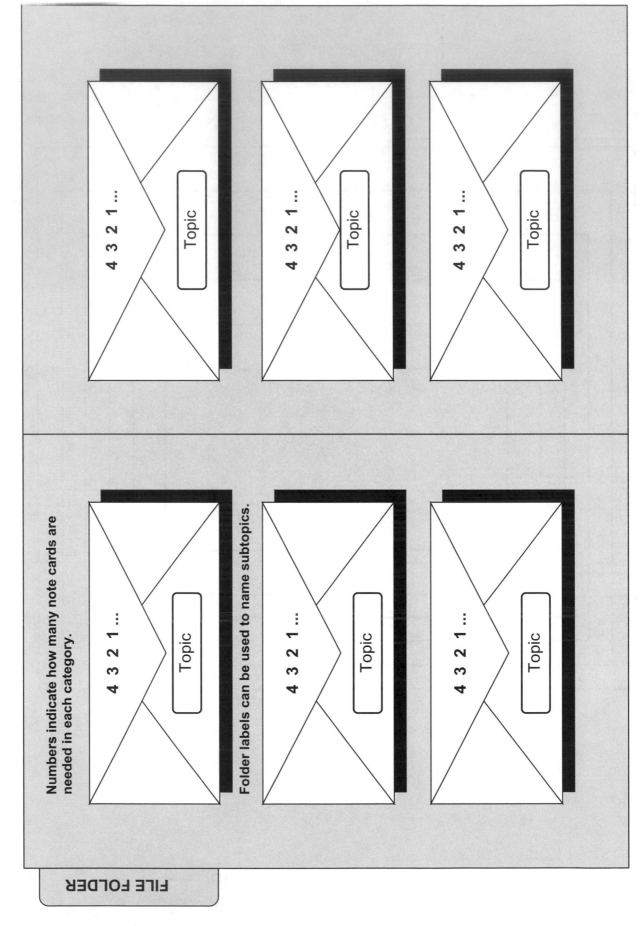

Numbers indicate how many note cards are needed in each category.

Folder labels can be used to name subtopics.

4 3 2 1...   Topic

FILE FOLDER

WHAT ☐   WHY ☑   HOW ☐

Mental Models in Math for Multiplication of Positive and Negative Numbers

+ Good guy − Bad guy	+ Coming to town − Leaving town	Get
+ + − −	+ − + −	+ − − +

☐ WHAT ☑ WHY ☐ HOW

Mental Models for Analogies

TYPES OF ANALOGIES

1. Synonyms

2. Antonyms

3. Indicative

4. Cause/effect

5. Subsets

6. Degree

7. Function/purpose

8. Definitional

****

VISUAL ANALOGY

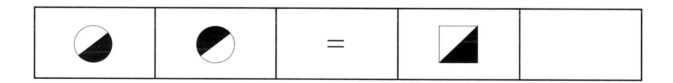

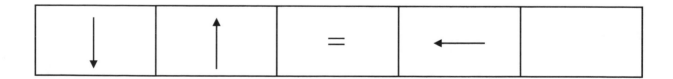

☐ WHAT ☑ WHY ☐ HOW

Mental Model of the Pythagorean Theorem

$$a^2+b^2=c^2$$

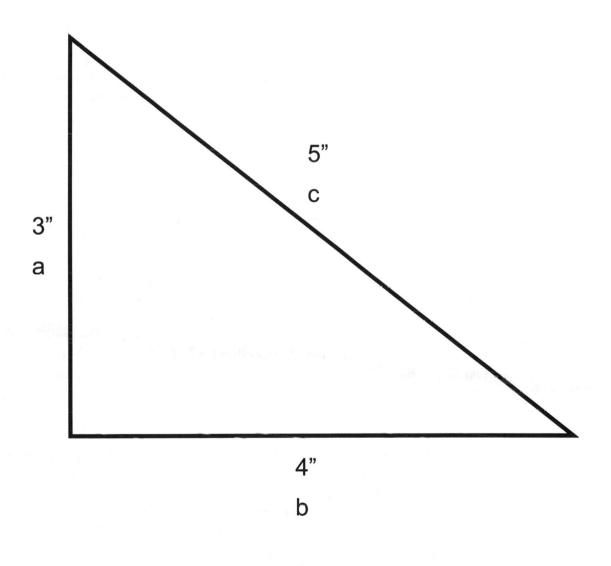

Planning to Control Impulsivity

There are several ways to teach impulse control to students. It is important to note that it's the student who does the planning, not the teacher. As long as the teacher does the planning, the student has not had to do the cognitive work. It's also important to note that, generally, planning is effective *only if the plan is written*.

1. **Planning Backwards** (p. 21). This method of planning has been very successful for many students. Draw a grid with a box for each day the student has before the assignment is due. Label the boxes with the days of the week and dates. Go to the last box—the day the project is due. Below the box make a list of tasks the students must do to finish the assignment. Then ask the students, "What do you have to do the day it is due?" Someone will say, "Hand it in." Then you ask, "What do you have to do the day before it is due?" and often you will get the very first thing that must be done. Eventually, you help the class pace the activities in such a way that the entire project can be done. Then the teacher gives grades two ways: One grade is given regarding the tasks completed each day and the other grade by the final product.

   Term paper planning (p. 22). is another example of planning a project, of planning backwards from a stated deadline.

2. **Plan, Do, Review** (p. 23). There are several variations on this method. Many teachers put the academic tasks on the board. The students keep a learning log. At the beginning of class they answer the question, "What is your plan for today?" They may write the order in which they are going to do the tasks or may say things like, "I am not going to talk to Robert today." At the end of class, they answer this question, "Did you do your plan? Why or why not?" For younger children, the plans can be in the form of drawn pictures.

3. **Step Sheets** (p. 24). Step sheets provide procedural information for academic tasks. If students cannot plan, they often do not have procedural self-talk. They tend to do the first few steps and then quit. A step sheet helps them successfully do the task—start to finish—every time.

4. **Planning Their Grades** (pp. 25-26). At the beginning of the grading period, the teacher asks students to answer questions about the kinds of grades they want. Then each Friday the teacher gives 15 minutes for the students to record their grades from the week, calculate their averages, and identify what they must do to maintain or bring up their grades.

5. **Pictures.** Especially for younger students, planning can be taught in the form of pictures. One picture can be of a student who did not plan and another of one who did. It can be as simple as one was happy because he had a plan and got to do what he wanted to do at recess. The other student did not have a plan and did not get to do what she wanted to do at recess. A plan helps you get what you want.

Mental Model for Time

Planning Backwards

Monday	Tuesday	Wednesday	Thursday	Friday

☐ WHAT ☑ WHY ☐ HOW

Term Paper Planning

Topic: _____

Length: _____

Numbers of sources:

Primary _____

Secondary _____

Steps →	→	→	→	→
Estimated time				
Target date				
Date assigned →	→	→	→	Deadline

Plan, Do, Review

PLAN FOR THE DAY	STEPS TO DO	REVIEW (HOW DID I DO?)

 ☐ WHAT ☑ WHY ☐ HOW

Step Sheet

STEPS	AMOUNT OF TIME
1.	
2.	
3.	
4.	
5.	
6.	
7.	
8.	
9.	
10.	
11.	
12.	

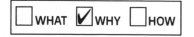
☐ WHAT ☑ WHY ☐ HOW

English III—Making the Grade

1. **What work have I done well in my English class?**

   a.

   b.

   c.

   d.

2. **What work have I done poorly in my English class?**

   a.

   b.

   c.

   d.

3. **I was/was not satisfied with my grade in English III last semester.**

   1st _____   2nd _____   3rd _____   Exam _____   Average _____

4. **What grade do I realistically believe that I can earn this semester in English III?** _____

5. **What will I do in my English class to earn that grade?**

   a.

   b.

   c.

WHAT	✔ WHY	HOW

Spring Semester

Fourth Grading Period   I want to earn _____.

Daily 10%   Quiz 30%   Test 60%

Fifth Grading Period   I want to earn _____.

Daily 10%   Quiz 30%   Test 60%

Sixth Grading Period   I want to earn _____.

Daily 10%   Quiz 30%   Test 60%

I am/am not satisfied with my grade in English III this semester.

1st _____   2nd _____   3rd _____   Exam _____   Average _____

☐ WHAT   ☑ WHY   ☐ HOW

MODULE 10

STRATEGIES FOR TEACHING THE *WHAT*

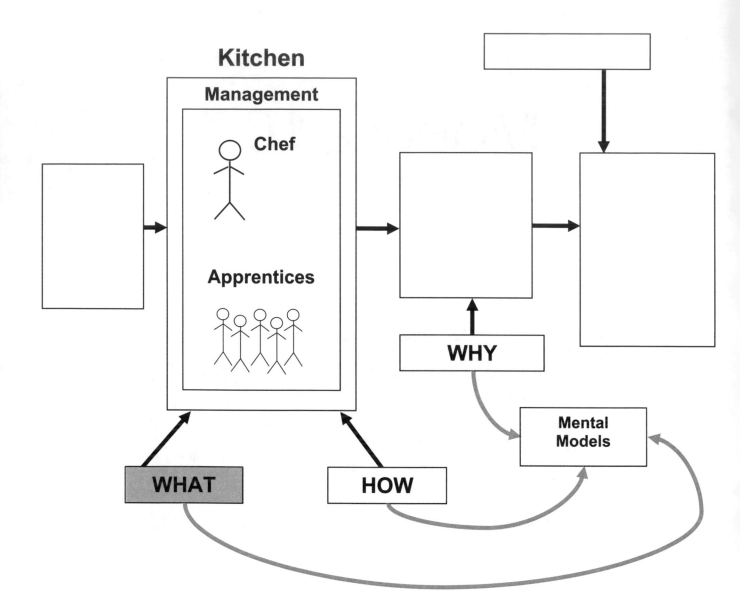

Full diagram in Appendix A, page 84

Vocabulary Strategies

#1 Knowledge Ratings

Using a graph like the one below, have students list the words in the first column to be studied. They evaluate their knowledge level of each word and check the appropriate box. If they have some idea of the meaning, they write in their guess. Following discussion or study, they write the definition in their own words. This activity is particularly useful in helping students develop metacognitive (being able to think about one's own thinking) awareness.

Example:

WORD	Know	Think I Know	Have Heard	GUESS	DEFINITION
saline			X	A liquid for contact lenses	A salt solution

Activity:

WORD	Know	Think I Know	Have Heard	GUESS	DEFINITION
torsade					
lurdane					
macula					

☑ WHAT ☐ WHY ☐ HOW

#2 Word Dangles

Students read a novel or story and then, on a piece of construction paper, illustrate it and write a summary of it. From the selection, they choose approximately five words that interest them, then write and illustrate each word on a separate card. They write a definition of the word on the reverse side of the card. The cards subsequently are attached to the bottom of the construction paper and "dangle" from it. The finished product can be hung as a mobile.

By using "word dangles," students enhance their comprehension. The illustrations also help them with conceptualization. They learn how vocabulary, reading, and writing are connected. The strategy is adaptable for all content areas, including fine arts. For example, in math, students might write a summary of a process and write, define, and illustrate several key words for that process. "Word dangles" also provide a word-rich environment and stimulate student interest in vocabulary study.

Example:

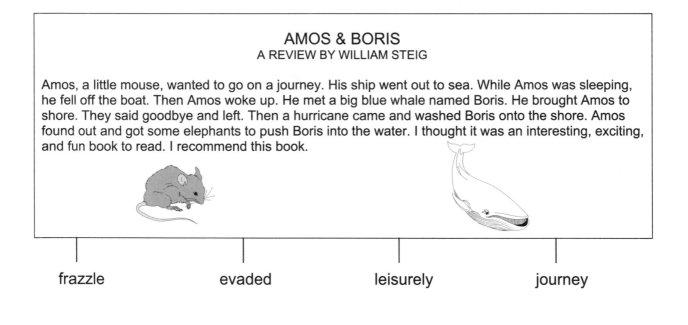

AMOS & BORIS
A REVIEW BY WILLIAM STEIG

Amos, a little mouse, wanted to go on a journey. His ship went out to sea. While Amos was sleeping, he fell off the boat. Then Amos woke up. He met a big blue whale named Boris. He brought Amos to shore. They said goodbye and left. Then a hurricane came and washed Boris onto the shore. Amos found out and got some elephants to push Boris into the water. I thought it was an interesting, exciting, and fun book to read. I recommend this book.

frazzle   evaded   leisurely   journey

☑ WHAT ☐ WHY ☐ HOW

```
+----------------------------------------------------------------------+
|                                                                      |
|                               TITLE                                  |
|                               Author                                 |
|                                                                      |
|                               Text                                   |
|                                                                      |
|                                                                      |
|            (picture)                          (picture)              |
|                                                                      |
|                                                                      |
+----------------------------------------------------------------------+
      |                 |                   |                 |
vocabulary word   vocabulary word   vocabulary word   vocabulary word
```

#3 Picture It

With each new story/reading, assign each student one vocabulary word. Students must:

- Find the word in the story/reading and record the page number (see form below).
- Find the word in the dictionary and record the pronunciation, number of syllables, part of speech, and definition used in the story.
- Create a picture of the word (on the second form below) to represent the word.
- Present the word to the class using the definition and picture.

Activity:

_____   _____

(word)   (page number)

_____   _____   _____

(pronunciation)   (# of syllables)   (part of speech)

Definition from story_____

_____

_____

Word picture

☑ WHAT ☐ WHY ☐ HOW

#4 Word Web

Students write the target word in the box, then write a synonym, an antonym, a definition, and an experience to complete the web.

Example:

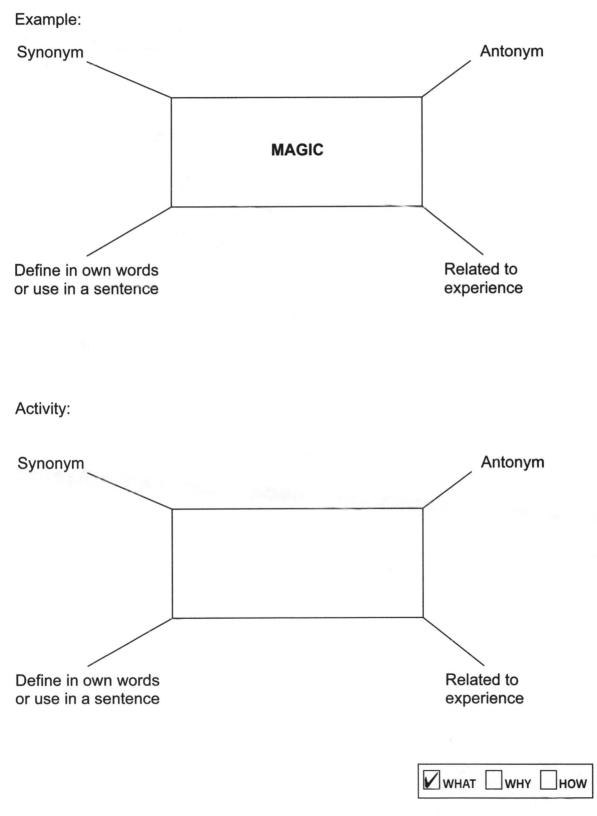

Synonym   Antonym

MAGIC

Define in own words
or use in a sentence

Related to
experience

Activity:

Synonym   Antonym

Define in own words
or use in a sentence

Related to
experience

☑ WHAT ☐ WHY ☐ HOW

#5 Concept Building

Guessing opposites or seeing relationships

To a small group, the teacher says:
1. Candy is sweet, but pickles are _____
2. An airplane is fast, but a horse is _____
3. The sky is above; the ground is _____

This type of procedure can also be used to elicit analogies.

Examples:

1. Pies are made by a baker; clothes are made by a _____
2. A cat runs on its legs, but a car runs on _____
3. In the morning the sun rises; at night the sun _____

The level at which this exercise can be done will vary widely with different children.

Activity:

1. _____
2. _____
3. _____

☑ WHAT ☐ WHY ☐ HOW

#6 Intermediate Adaptation

With each text reading, assign each student one vocabulary word. Students must do the following:

- Find the word in the text.
- Copy text definition (taken directly from book).
- Write own definition (in student's own words).
- Use discriminating/distinguishing characteristics (information that helps to give more details about the word).
- Draw illustration (drawing that gives a visual representation of the word).

Example:

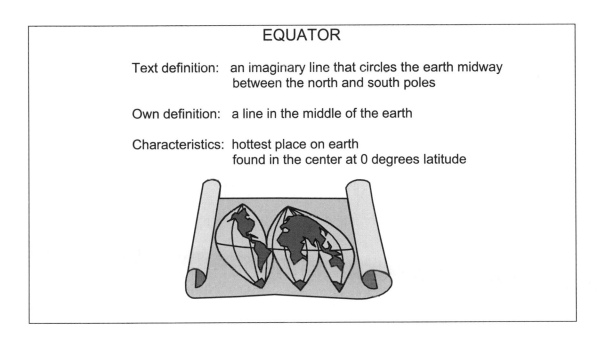

EQUATOR

Text definition: an imaginary line that circles the earth midway between the north and south poles

Own definition: a line in the middle of the earth

Characteristics: hottest place on earth
found in the center at 0 degrees latitude

☑ WHAT ☐ WHY ☐ HOW

Activity:

Materials needed: text reading, vocabulary list, teacher-developed worksheet

Vocabulary Word Map

DEFINITION or SYNONYM

ANTONYM

_____

VOCABULARY WORD

USE IT IN A SENTENCE

_____

_____

_____

_____

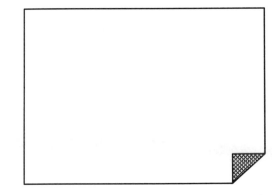

DRAW A PICTURE or RELATE IT TO YOURSELF

Adapted from materials of Raymond C. Jones, found at www.readingquest.org

☑ WHAT ☐ WHY ☐ HOW

MODULE 11

STRATEGIES FOR TEACHING THE *How*

Kitchen

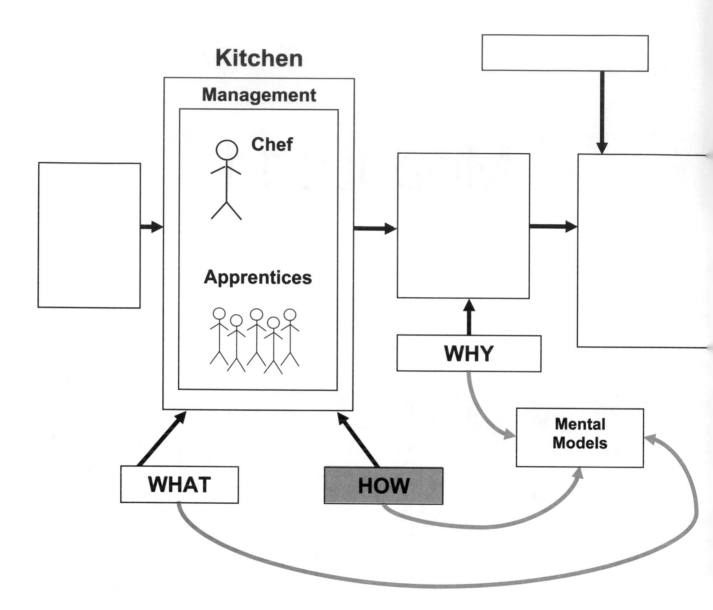

Full diagram in Appendix A, page 84

Cognitive Strategies

**INPUT:
Quantity and
quality of
data gathered**

1. Use planning behaviors.
2. Focus perception on specific stimulus.
3. Control impulsivity.
4. Explore data systematically.
5. Use appropriate and accurate labels.
6. Organize space using stable systems of reference.
7. Orient data in time.
8. Identify constancies across variations.
9. Gather precise and accurate data.
10. Consider two sources of information at once.
11. Organize data (parts of a whole.)
12. Visually transport data.

1. Identify and define the problem.
2. Select relevant cues.
3. Compare data.
4. Select appropriate categories of time.
5. Summarize data.
6. Project relationship of data.
7. Use logical data.
8. Test hypothesis.
9. Build inferences.
10. Make a plan using the data.
11. Use appropriate labels.
12. Use data systematically.

**ELABORATION:
Efficient use of data**

**OUTPUT:
Communication
of elaboration
and input**

1. Communicate clearly the labels and processes.
2. Visually transport data correctly.
3. Use precise and accurate language.
4. Control impulsive behavior.

Adapted from work of Reuven Feuerstein

Plan and Label for Academic Tasks

There are at least four ways to *systematically label* tasks: numbering, lettering, assigning symbols, and color-coding. It is important to note that a systematic approach to the labeling means that fewer pieces of the task are skipped or missed.

For a task to be done correctly, a student must have:
- *a plan*
- *a procedure*
- *labels (vocabulary). Labels are the tools the mind uses to address the task.*

There are several ways to teach this. It's easier to begin by using visual activities that have no words. This teaches students that all tasks must have a plan and labels.

1. Use symbols to label: problem-solving process (p. 43) or in division (p. 44).

2. Plan and label: identifying characteristics (p. 45).

3. Plan and Label Space (p. 46).

4. Plan and label text: have the students sketch a process, such as the making of a battery (p. 47).

5. Plan and label text: reading strategies (pp. 48-50). Have students outline the left-hand edge of text. (You can copy a page of text from a textbook or give them clear transparency sheets to lay over the text.) When the paragraph indents, the student indents. Wherever the line indents, students number inside the indent. Then students find the one word that tells what that paragraph is about and circle it. It becomes a very quick referencing system and also can become a way to summarize. Students are asked to write one sentence with each circled word. The sentences become a summary of the text. This is also an example of using symbols.

6. Develop specific vocabulary and symbols with specific tasks, as in classificatory writing (p. 51).

www.ahaprocess.com

Problem-Solving Process

Step 1: READ THE PROBLEM

- Read the problem through completely to get a general idea of what the problem is asking.

Step 2: REREAD THE PROBLEM AND QUESTION

- Reread to visualize the problem.
- Highlight or mark the question with a wavy line.

Step 3: MARK YOUR INFORMATION

- Mark the important information and eliminate unnecessary information.

- Box the action or important words.

- Circle needed information.

- Loop out extra information. *eeeeee*

Step 4: CHOOSE AN APPROPRIATE STRATEGY

- Choose an operation (+ - x ÷).
- Solve a simpler problem.
- Make an organized list.
- Look for a pattern.
- Use logical reasoning.
- Guess and check.
- Make a table.
- Use objects.
- Draw a picture.
- Act it out.
- Work backwards.

Step 5: SOLVE

- Solve the problem.

Step 6: IS THE QUESTION ANSWERED?

- Read the question again.
- Does the solution answer the question?
- Does it make sense? Is it reasonable?
- Check by using a different strategy if possible.

Source: Judy Sain, Daily Math Skills Review

Plan and Label in Math

1. 6⟌	Divisor: number of parts in a group
2. ⟌240	Dividend: total number of parts
3. ⟌	Quotient: number of groups
4. 6⟌240	Are there enough parts for a group?
5. 6⟌240	Are there enough parts for a group? If so, how many groups?
6. x 4 / 6⟌24 / 24	See if there are extra parts.

☐ WHAT ☐ WHY ☑ HOW

Plan and Label: Identifying Characteristics

Look at the sample. In each of the two frames, make a new drawing using the changes indicated.

	number color size form	number color size form
	number color size form	number color size form
	number color size form	number color size form
	number color size form	number color size form
	number color size form	number color size form
	number color size form	number color size form

☐ WHAT ☐ WHY ☑ HOW

Plan and Label Space

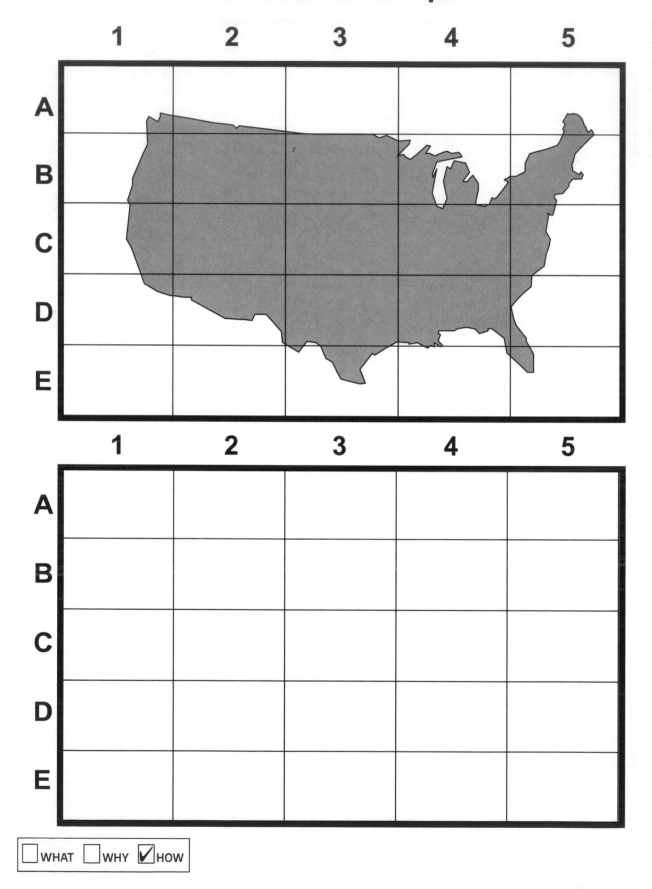

☐ WHAT ☐ WHY ☑ HOW

Plan and Label in Science

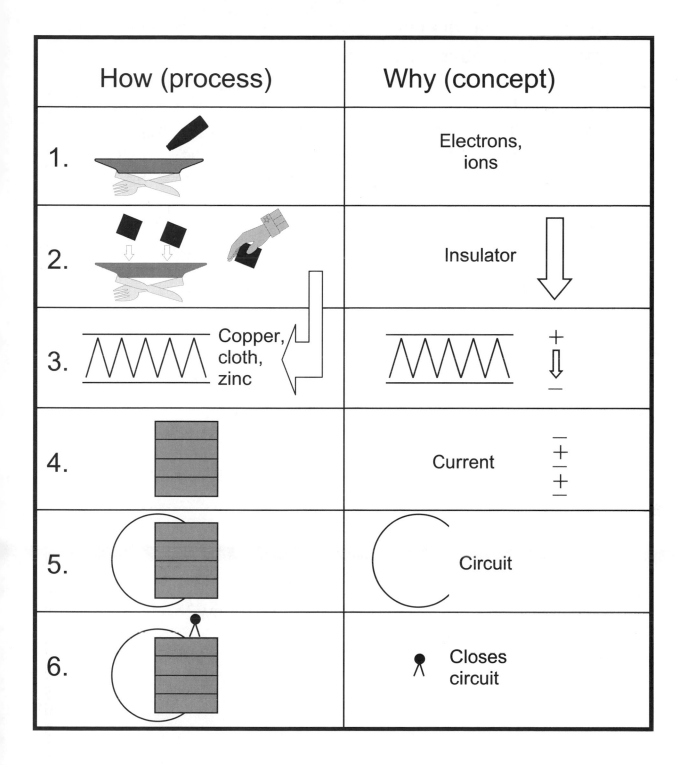

How (process)	Why (concept)
1.	Electrons, ions
2.	Insulator
3. Copper, cloth, zinc	
4.	Current
5.	Circuit
6.	Closes circuit

Reading Strategies

1. Box in and read the title.
2. Trace and number the paragraphs.
3. Stop and think at the end of each paragraph to identify a key point.
4. Circle the key word or write the key point in the margin.
5. Read and label the key words in the questions.
6. Prove your answer. Locate the paragraph where the answer is found.
7. Mark or write your answer.

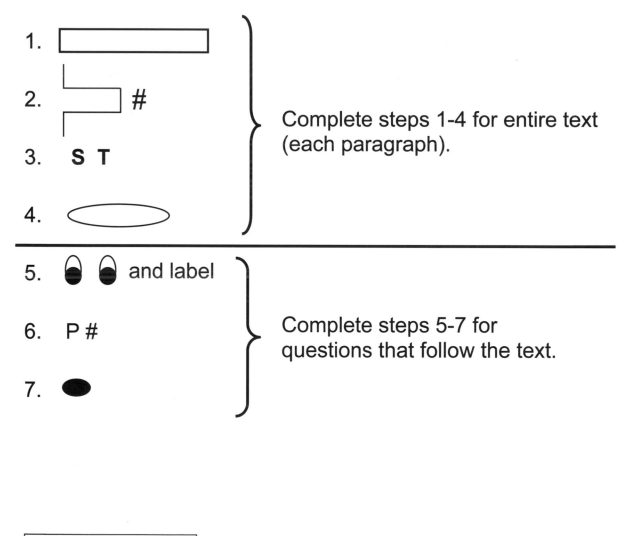

1.

2. #

3. S T

4.

Complete steps 1-4 for entire text (each paragraph).

5. and label

6. P #

7.

Complete steps 5-7 for questions that follow the text.

☐ WHAT   ☐ WHY   ☑ HOW

The Little Armored One

The armadillo is a peculiar-looking animal. Its unusual appearance is more like that of a dinosaur than of a mammal living today. In fact, the armadillo is a cousin to some prehistoric animals. However, the armadillo is in little danger of going the way of its extinct relatives. The armadillo population is growing, and the armadillo is actually <u>extending</u> the range of places where it lives. Formerly found mainly in Mexico and South America, this fascinating animal traveled north and east and now lives in Texas, Louisiana, and Oklahoma. Its range is limited only by the frost line, for the armadillo is not suited to cold weather.

The word *armadillo* is Spanish for "little armored one." The animal gets its name from its outer shell. This armored shell is made up of separate plates, which allow the armadillo to curl up into a tight ball and protect its soft underbelly if threatened. This response is a last resort, for the armadillo can usually <u>elude</u> its enemies. It is a very fast runner and strong digger; if it does not outrun its enemies, it can usually burrow to safety.

The little armored one is not a fussy eater. It likes to eat such delicacies as angleworms and cutworms. It has poor vision, so it uses its sharp sense of smell to sniff the bugs out and then digs for them with its nose.

The armadillo's appetite is <u>immense</u>. An armadillo can eat more than 100 cutworms in a single day. Some people believe the effectiveness of the little armored one as a pest controller can outweigh any negative effect its digging may have on garden crops.

One of the most unusual characteristics of the armadillo is the way it crosses water. Since it can hold its breath for as long as six minutes, the armadillo will walk across the bottom of a narrow stream or river. It crosses wider rivers by swallowing air into its stomach and intestines and then floating or paddling across. If the river is moving fast, the little animal will grab hold of pieces of floating wood to help it get to the other side of the river.

The armadillo is harmless and beneficial, interesting and unusual. Some of the characteristics that make it different from other animals have also helped the armadillo to thrive.

Taken from Texas Assessment of Academic Skills (1996) Grade 5

1. Why might a gardener <u>not</u> want an armadillo in the garden?

   A   An armadillo sometimes damages vegetables as it digs for insects.
   B   An armadillo often attacks gardeners.
   C   An armadillo gives birth in vegetable gardens.
   D   An armadillo attracts bugs that damage garden crops.

2. The word <u>extending</u> in this passage means

   F   surviving.
   G   protecting.
   H   restricting.
   J   increasing.

3. You can tell from the passage that the armadillo

   A   uses its sharp eyesight to find food.
   B   cannot cross large rivers or streams.
   C   has been able to adapt to its surroundings.
   D   does not have any natural enemies.

4. What is the main idea of the second paragraph?

   F   The armadillo's shell is its only protection against enemies.
   G   The armadillo is most often found curled up in a tight ball.
   H   The armadillo has strong claws to dig deep holes.
   J   The armadillo has several ways to protect itself from enemies.

5. According to the passage, it is likely that in the future the armadillo population will

   A   become extinct.
   B   increase in number.
   C   move to colder climates.
   D   develop soft outer shells.

6. In this passage, <u>elude</u> means to

   F   escape.
   G   kill.
   H   fight.
   J   assist.

7. Which is the best summary of the passage?

   A   The armadillo is found mainly in Mexico and South America.
   B   The armadillo has special characteristics that have helped it to survive.
   C   The armadillo has a very unusual diet.
   D   The armadillo is a relative of some prehistoric animals.

8. In this passage, <u>immense</u> means

   F   ancient.
   G   destructive.
   H   enormous.
   J   wasteful.

9. An armadillo swallows air because it

   A   makes a noise that frightens the armadillo's enemies.
   B   lets the armadillo eat less food.
   C   increases the armadillo's sense of smell.
   D   helps the armadillo to float.

Taken from Texas Assessment of Academic Skills (1996) Grade 5

Classificatory Writing

Paragraph 1 **INTRODUCTION**
- 3+ sentences.
- Rewrite the prompt.
- Give general information and/or an opinion.

Paragraph 2 **ADVANTAGES**
- 8+ sentences.
- Make a statement: "There are advantages to ..."
- Write *ADV 1* sentence.
- *Elaborate* using two sentences.
- Write *ADV 2* sentence.
- *Elaborate* using two sentences.
- Make a concluding statement: "There are some advantages to ..."

Paragraph 3 **ADVANTAGES OR DISADVANTAGES**
- 8+ sentences.
- Make a statement: "Additionally, there are other advantages to ..." or "On the other hand, there are disadvantages to ..."
- Write *ADV 3 or DIS 1* sentence.
- *Elaborate* using two sentences.
- Write *ADV 4 or DIS 2* sentence.
- *Elaborate* using two sentences.
- Make a concluding statement.

Paragraph 4 **DISADVANTAGES**
- 8+ sentences.
- Make a statement.
- Write *DIS 3 or DIS 1* sentence.
- *Elaborate* using two sentences.
- Write *DIS 4 or DIS 2* sentence.
- *Elaborate* using two sentences.
- Make a concluding statement.

Paragraph 5 **CONCLUSION**
- 3+ sentences.
- Restate the prompt.
- Give specific information and/or opinions.

Developed by Molly Davis and Julie Heffner

Sorting Information
Using Patterns and Criteria

To store and retrieve information, one must be able to sort using criteria. If the patterns are known, however, one can sort faster. Because children from poverty often come into school behind, ways are needed to teach information much faster. Teaching patterns as a way to sort is one way to shorten the time needed to teach something.

The mind sorts data against patterns, mental mindsets, and paradigms to determine what is "important" and what is not.

Items with the same attributes are assigned to a group.

Patterns can be identified using groups.

Abstract constructs are essential for grouping and patterning; these are necessary for success in school.

Here are some ways to teach sorting with the use of criteria and patterns.

1. Sorting M & M's. (Color may not be used as a criterion.)

2. Using patterns and models to sort (pp. 54-55).

3. Cartooning (p. 56). Use this form to cartoon the main events in a story.

4. Identifying the criteria used to group or sort (pp. 57-62).

Developing Sorting Strategies

The mind sorts data against patterns, mental mindsets, and paradigms to determine what is "important" and what is not.

Attributes become a sort of screen that allows "important" data to continue and stops "unimportant" data.

By teaching patterns within data, students can find what is "important" more quickly and accurately.

Identifying Characteristics

Using the column on the left, identify how the examples to the right are alike and different from the column on the left. Circle the words that indicate the way(s) in which the examples to the right are the same.

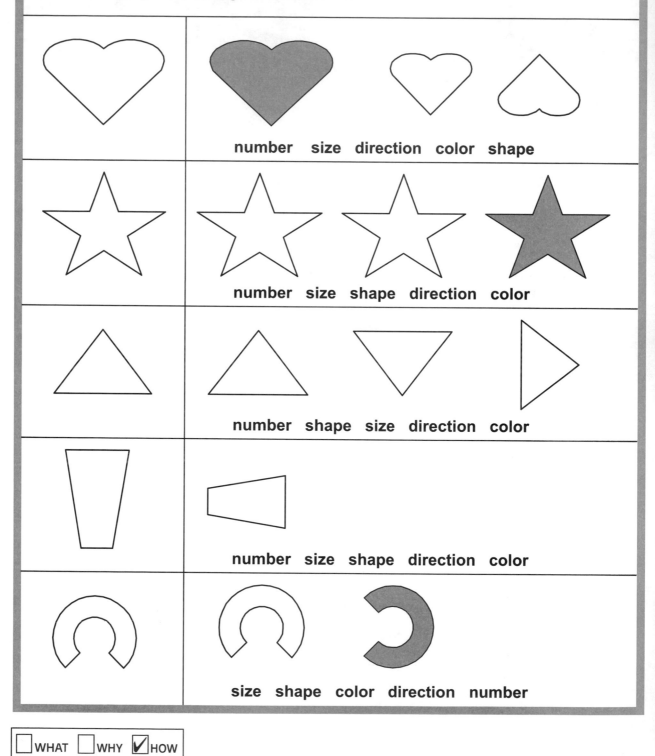

number   size   direction   color   shape

number   size   shape   direction   color

number   shape   size   direction   color

number   size   shape   direction   color

size   shape   color   direction   number

☐ WHAT   ☐ WHY   ☑ HOW

Identifying Characteristics

In the first column, write what the words have in common. In the second column, write how the words are different.

Words	Alike	Different
Sugar Salt		
Day Night		
Paper Pencil		
Car Truck		
Now Later		
Here There		
Tall Short		

☐ WHAT ☐ WHY ☑ HOW

Sorting by Criteria and Patterns

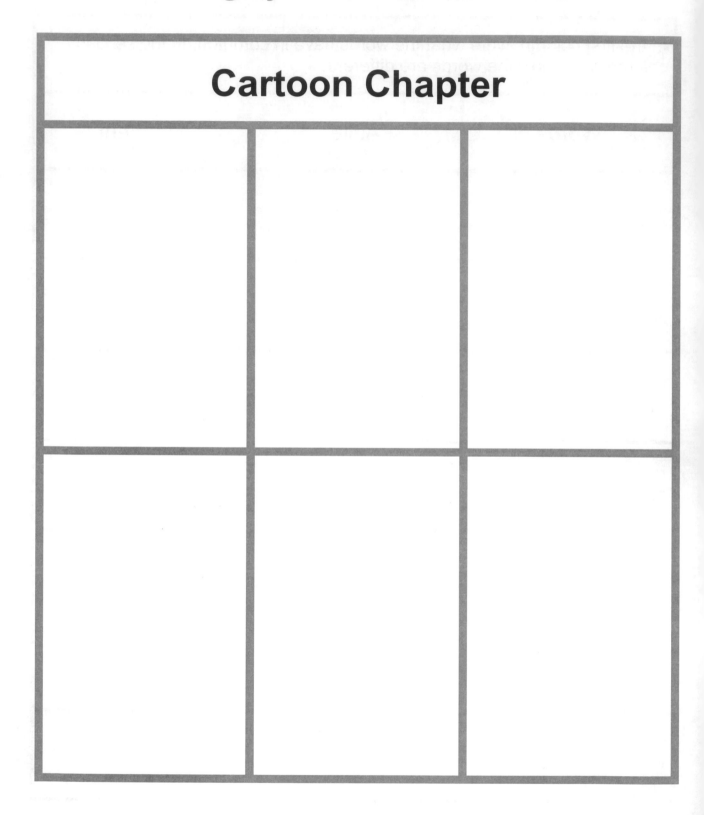

Cartoon Chapter

WHAT WHY ✔HOW

Five Models to Use
for Sorting

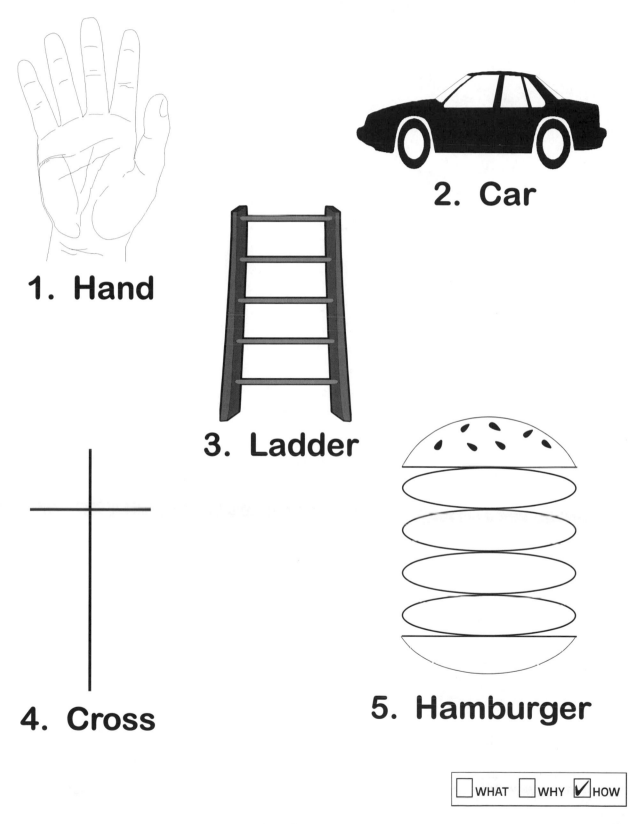

1. Hand

2. Car

3. Ladder

4. Cross

5. Hamburger

☐ WHAT ☐ WHY ☑ HOW

Descriptive/Topical

☐ WHAT ☐ WHY ☑ HOW

www.ahaprocess.com

Sequence/How-to

Story Structure

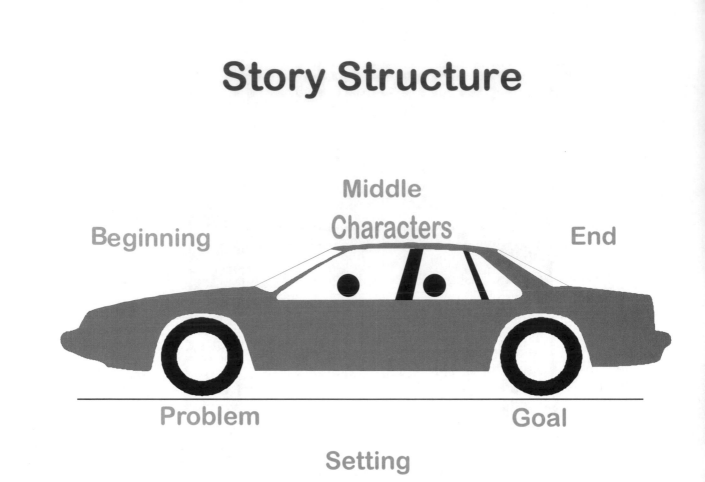

Beginning   Middle   Characters   End

Problem   Goal

Setting

☐ WHAT   ☐ WHY   ☑ HOW

Compare/Contrast
Advantages/Disadvantages
Cause/Effect

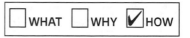

Persuasive Reasons

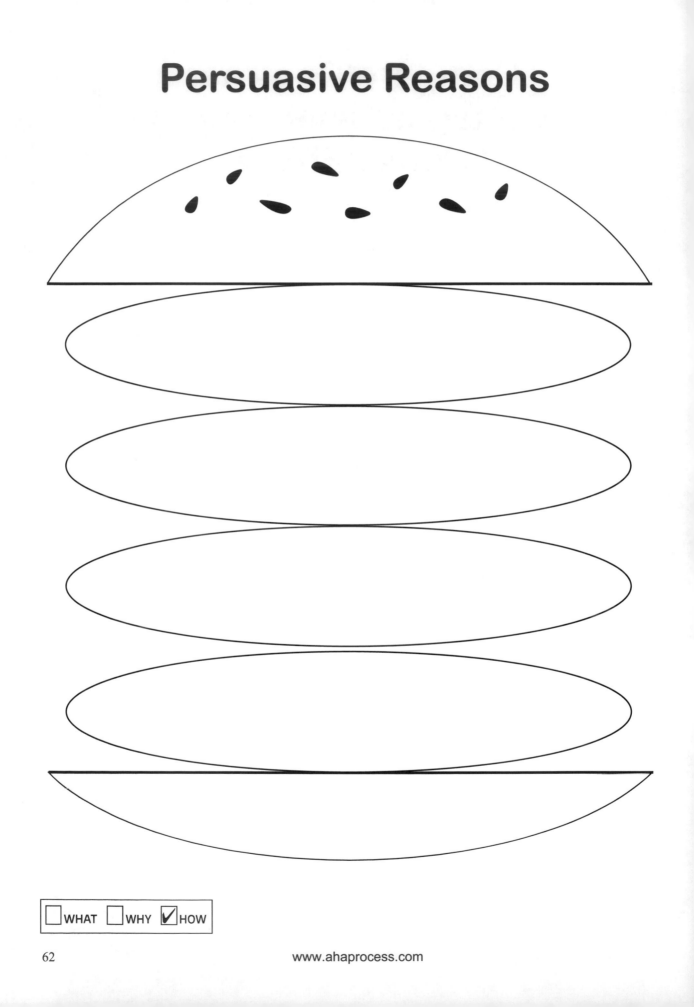

WHAT ☐ WHY ☐ HOW ✓

www.ahaprocess.com

Question Making

To be able to formulate questions syntactically is very important because without this ability the mind literally cannot know what it knows. Many students will ask questions through their tone of voice (e.g., "You don't have any more????"). That is a statement that the voice tone has made into a question. If they cannot examine their own behavior, then the students syntactically or grammatically make it into a question (e.g., "Don't you have any more?"). Or they ask it in the formal register of their native language.

To do any task, one must be able to go inside the head and ask questions. If individuals cannot, then they cannot examine any behavior, nor can they retrieve information in a systematic way. For example, if a teacher says to a student, "Why did you do that?" and the student replies, "I don't know," then the teacher needs to see if the student can ask questions syntactically or in formal register. Chances are very good that the student is saying to himself inside his head, "I did that?"

One of the most important cognitive skills to give to students is having them ask the questions. There are several ways to do this, including:

1. Play "Jeopardy!" This exercise involves you giving the answer, and the student needs to come up with the question.

2. For young students, have them start the first word of a sentence with one of the following words: who, what, when, where, which, how.

3. Have students write their own questions with multiple-choice answers (p. 64).

4. Use question stems for reading, math, and science (pp. 65-68).

5. Using a multiple-choice test, have students tell you why the incorrect answers are wrong. (While this doesn't give students the ability to ask questions syntactically, it does teach them how to identify wrong answers.)

Writing Multiple-Choice Questions

Question:

a.

b.

c.

d.

Three Rules:

1. One wrong-answer choice must be funny.

2. Only one answer choice can be right.

3. May not use "all of the above," "none of the above," etc.

Math Questions

1. Stems need to use the terminology.

2. Distracters are:

   - Incorrect operation

   - Incorrect order

   - Decimal in wrong place

   - Answer in wrong form (percentage instead of number, etc.)

   - Missed step

   - Unnecessary information included

   - Computational errors

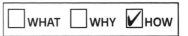

Reading-Objective Question Stems

Objective 1: Word Meaning

In this story the word _____ means …

The word _____ in this passage means …

Objective 2: Supporting Ideas

What did _____ do after …?

What happened just before _____ …?

What did _____ do first? Last?

According to the directions given, what was _____ supposed to do first?
After _____? Last?

Where does this story take place?

When does the story take place?

Objective 3: Summarizing Written Texts

Which sentence tells the main idea of the story?

This story is mainly about …

What is the main idea of paragraph 3?

What is the story mostly about?

Which statement best summarizes this passage? (paragraph)

Objective 4: Perceiving Relationships and Recognizing Outcomes

Why did __(name)__ do __(action)__?

What will happen as a result of _____?

Based on the information, which is _____ most likely to do?

What will happen to _____ in this story?

You can tell from this passage that _____ is most likely to …

Objective 5: Analyzing Information to Make Inference and Generalization

How did _____ feel about _____?

How does _____ feel at the beginning (end) of the story?

According to Figure 1, what …? (where, how many, when)

The __(event)__ is being held in order to …

By __(action)__, __(name)__ was able to show that …

You can tell from this passage that …?

Which word best describes _____'s feelings in this passage?

Objective 6: Distinguishing Between Fact and Opinion

Which of these is a fact expressed in the passage?

Which of these is an opinion expressed in the passage?

☐ WHAT ☐ WHY ☑ HOW

Science Question Stems
Ninth Grade

1. The chart shows _____. Which of these would complete the column?
2. The chart (graph) shows _____. According to the information, how many (how much) _____?
3. What would happen if …?
4. What tool is used to find _____?
5. The picture shows the process of …?
6. Which tools are needed to find how mass affects the distance these _____ will _____?
7. Which of these questions can be answered from the results of the experiment?
8. If … then which will most likely occur?
9. What process is taking place?
10. Which experiment will best show …? (four pictures given)
11. Which of these best represents …? (diagram given)
12. What conclusion can be drawn from this graph?
13. In the diagram, the label Z represents …
14. This experiment was probably set up to answer which of the following questions? (picture given)
15. What is the mass of these _____?

Adapted from TAKS (Texas Assessment of Knowledge and Skills)

☐ WHAT ☐ WHY ☑ HOW

Question Stems
Fifth- and Ninth-Grade Reading

1. In paragraph _____, what does _____ mean?
2. Paragraph _____ is mainly about _____.
3. From the article, the reader can tell …
4. From the passage, the reader can tell …
5. From the paragraph, the reader can tell …
6. From what the reader learns about _____, which statement does not make sense?
7. How does _____ feel?
8. Why is it important …?
9. Which of these is the best summary of the selection?
10. Look at this web (flow chart, graph, charts, etc.). Which detail belongs in the empty space?
11. An idea present in both selections is …
12. One way these selections are alike is …
13. One way these selections are different is …
14. Paragraph _____ is important because it helps the reader understand …
15. The reader can tell when _____, he/she will probably …
16. How does _____ feel?
17. In paragraph _____, why is _____ sad? (happy, confused, angry, etc.)
18. What is this article mainly about?
19. What can the reader tell about _____ from information in this article?
20. The author builds suspense by …
21. One way this story resembles a fable is that …
22. In paragraph _____, the author uses the word _____ to emphasize—
23. Which of the following words is a synonym (antonym) for the word _____ in paragraph _____?
24. What is the overall theme expressed in this article?
25. Which of the following sentences from the article explains the author's primary conflict?
26. The audience that would probably relate most to the article's central message would be …
27. Why …?
28. How ...?

Adapted from TAKS (Texas Assessment of Knowledge and Skills)

☐ WHAT ☐ WHY ☑ HOW

MODULE 12

PUTTING IT ALL TOGETHER: LESSON DESIGN

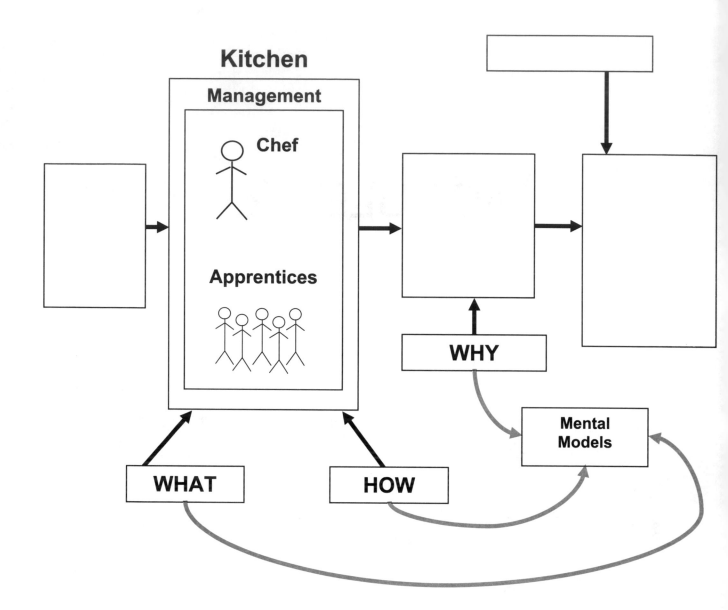

Kitchen

Management

Chef

Apprentices

WHY

Mental Models

WHAT

HOW

Full diagram in Appendix A, page 84

SCIENCE JOURNAL

By SHARON BEGLEY

Diet During Pregnancy Could Have Effects That Last to Adulthood

AS MYSTERIES GO, these don't seem to have much in common: A child born underweight has a higher than normal risk of developing heart disease, diabetes, obesity and hypertension as an adult. One identical twin develops schizophrenia, which studies of families show is a genetic disease, but the other twin is spared.

Last week's column looked at scientists' growing realization that, when it comes to important changes in the genome—if I may corrupt an old political mantra—"it's not just the sequence, stupid." Mice with identical genes for fur color can be brownish or yellow, depending on whether their gene for fur color has been silenced by what their mother ate during pregnancy. It's beginning to look as if such "epigenetic" changes, defined as those having no effect on the sequence of molecules that make up a genome, may be major players in determining traits and disease risk.

"The completion of the human genome project is a monumental event, but there's still an enormous amount that we have not yet

Gordon Studer

fleshed out," says psychiatrist James Potash of Johns Hopkins University School of Medicine, Baltimore. "Epigenetic variation is one."

TAKE THE ENIGMA of fetal programming, in which nutrition during gestation seems to affect the risk of disease decades later. At a June conference on the subject, attended by some 700 scientists, "What came shining through is that birth weight affects the risk of diabetes, coronary heart disease, obesity, hypertension and breast or prostate cancers," says David Barker of England's University of Southampton. Scrawny newborns, in general, grow up to have a higher incidence of the first four; chubby ones, a higher risk of the latter.

At first, scientists thought the reason was physiology, not genetics. For example, newborns who are small for their length probably have fewer kidney cells than they should. Since the kidneys regulate blood pressure, undersized kidneys can increase later risk of hypertension and thus heart disease, explains Dr. Barker.

But fetal programming "almost certainly" reflects epigenetic changes, too, says Craig Cooney of the University of Arkansas for Medical Sciences. That's because, much as in the mice whose color reflects what mom ate while pregnant, nutrients reaching the human fetus can include more or fewer of the molecules that silence or activate genes. Maybe too few nutrients during gestation might mean not enough of the molecules that silence heart-disease-causing genes.

"The nutrition an embryo receives at crucial stages of development can have important and lasting effects on the expression of various genes, including those involved in health and disease," says Randy Jirtle of Duke University Medical Center, Durham, N.C.

One target of such silencing must have Gregor Mendel turning over in his grave. The Austrian monk, regarded as the founder of genetics, concluded that which parent a gene comes from is irrelevant. True, we carry two copies of every gene (except those on the Y chromosome), one from mom and one from dad. But dozens of genes in sperm or ova are tagged with the biochemical equivalent of "don't mind me." Throughout life, those genes are silenced, or "imprinted." If mom's gene is imprinted, only dad's counts; if dad's is imprinted, only mom's counts.

THE GENE SEQUENCE hasn't changed, so imprinting is epigenetic—and something you don't want to mess up. When the gene for insulin-like growth factor 2 (IGF2) loses its imprinting, for instance, the once-silenced copy is activated, loosing a flood of growth factor that promotes childhood and adult cancers. Yet if you were to sequence that IGF2 gene, it would look just fine.

Such imprinting mistakes may be affecting some test-tube babies. The incidence of a rare genetic disease called Beckwith-Wiedemann syndrome was six times as high as in children conceived the traditional way, according to a study published in January. This syndrome occurs when IGF2 loses its "keep quiet" marker.

"There is reason to believe, from animal studies, that assisted-reproductive technology can lead to more frequent imprinting errors," says Hopkins geneticist Andrew Feinberg. One suspect: the broth in which ova and embryos grow before being implanted in the mother's womb. It may somehow unsilence imprinted genes.

Epigenetics might also solve the puzzle of identical twins who do not have the same "genetic" diseases, especially psychiatric ones. "You wonder if the difference might be that something causes a gene related to mental illness to be silenced in one twin but not the other," says Dr. Potash.

In the old joke, a drunk searches for his lost keys under a streetlight, not because he dropped them there, but because the light is good. The search for genetic variants—differences in DNA sequences—underlying complex diseases is starting to look like that. Sequence variants are easy to find: the light's good there, so scientists have found more than a million sequence variants. But they don't correspond too well with genetically based complex diseases. No wonder the spotlight is turning from genetics to epigenetics, the pattern of gene silencing and activation.

You can e-mail me at sciencejournal@wsj.com.

Source: WALL STREET JOURNAL. MIDWEST EDITION [STAFF PRODUCED COPY ONLY] by SHARON BEGLEY. Copyright 2003 by DOW JONES & CO INC. Reproduced with permission of DOW JONES & CO INC in the format Textbook via Copyright Clearance Center.

Payne Lesson Design

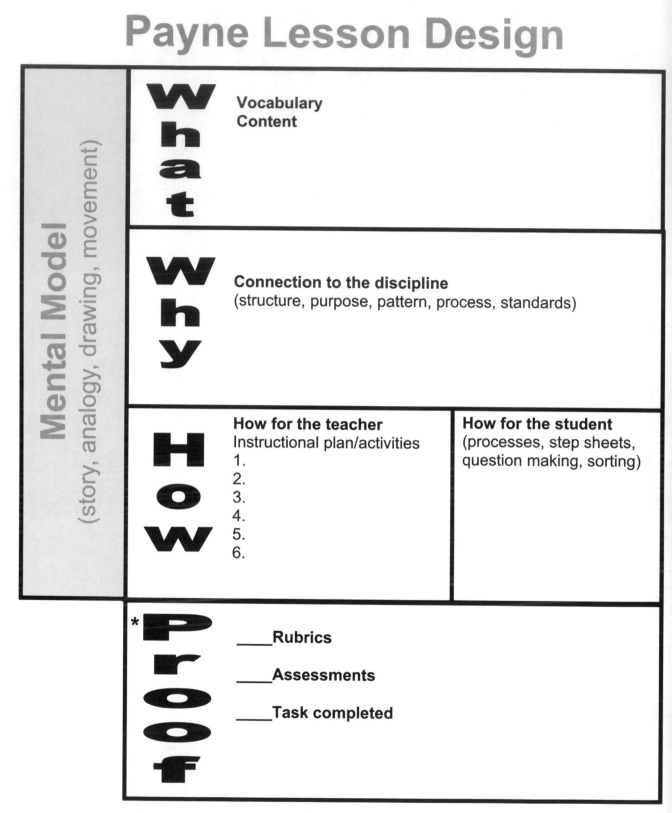

Mental Model
(story, analogy, drawing, movement)

What
Vocabulary
Content

Why
Connection to the discipline
(structure, purpose, pattern, process, standards)

How

How for the teacher
Instructional plan/activities
1.
2.
3.
4.
5.
6.

How for the student
(processes, step sheets,
question making, sorting)

*Proof

____Rubrics

____Assessments

____Task completed

* This should be shared with students.

Payne Lesson Design

Mental Model
(story, analogy, drawing, movement)

What

Vocabulary
Content

Epigenetic, fetal programming, gene silencing, genetic variants, imprinting

Why

Connection to the Discipline
(structure, purpose, pattern, process, standards)
Standard knowledge of biological concepts

How

Instructional plan/activities

1. Plan and label text.
2. Put "v" above new vocabulary.
3. Discuss vocabulary.
4. Write questions.
5. Choose "proof."

Process:
Do question making in pairs; have students write one question over the article

Steps students need to take to do the tasks

1. Label text.
2. Read article.
3. Put "v" above new vocabulary.

*Proof

____Rubrics
____Assessments
____Task completed

Summarize article using five vocabulary words.
Write letter to your sister explaining importance of her diet; use five words.
Sketch five vocabulary words.
Go online; find and print two additional articles on epigenetics.
Develop your own drawing.

* This should be shared with students.

Epigenetics: Patterns of Gene Silencing and Activation

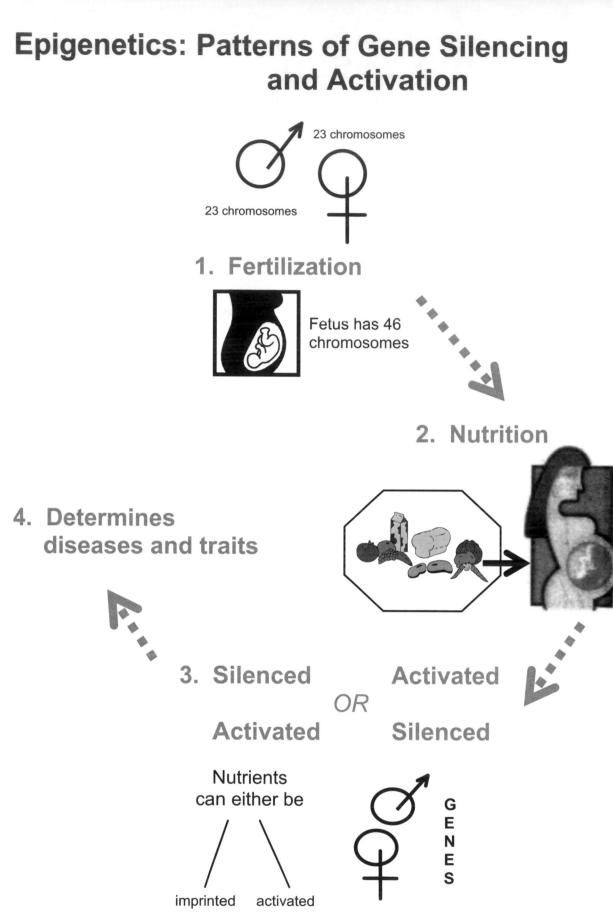

23 chromosomes

23 chromosomes

1. Fertilization

Fetus has 46 chromosomes

2. Nutrition

4. Determines diseases and traits

3. Silenced   Activated

OR

Activated   Silenced

Nutrients can either be

imprinted   activated

(silent)

G E N E S

MODULE 13

ASSESSMENT
(Optional)

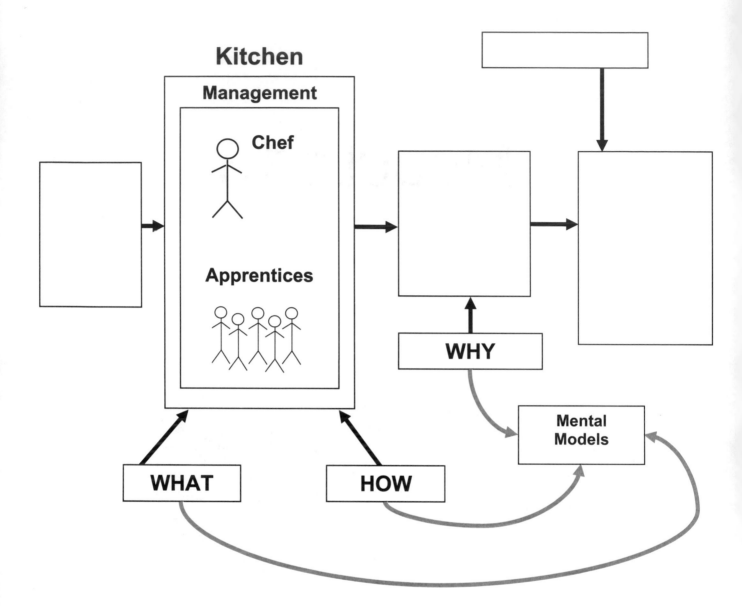

Full diagram in Appendix A, page 84

Question Analysis Form

QUESTION	YES	NO	COMMENTS
1. Does the question go with the standard?			
2. Is there a correct answer?			
3. Is there more than one correct answer?			
4. Does the answer go with the question?			
5. Does the question discriminate by race, gender, age, or economic class?			
6. Are the wrong answer choices (distractors) appropriate for the question?			
7. Does the stem mirror the state assessment?			
8. Is the question too specific to a particular kind or aspect of information?			
9. Does the question assess in the same manner the students are taught?			
10. Is the readability appropriate for the grade level assessed?			
11. Is the difficulty of the passage (vocabulary, concept, sentence complexity, topic) appropriate for the grade level?			
12. Is the vocabulary/terminology used in instruction?			
13. Is the stem (question part of the question) clearly phrased?			
14. Is this question a part of any unit that is taught?			
15. Does this question require prior knowledge?			
16. What is the P value of this question?			
17. Is the question formatted appropriately?			
18. Are the directions clear?			

Question Analysis

1. Jake made a map of his neighborhood for a school project. He placed a grid over the map.

   Which coordinate point best represents Jake's house?

   A. (12,10)
   B. (10,12)
   C. (1, 1.2)
   D. (1.2, 1)

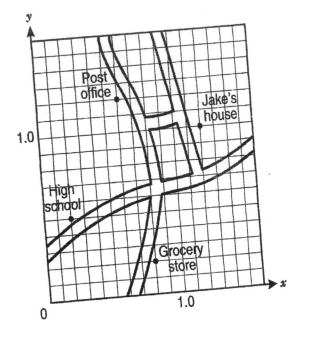

2. In the diagram, the label Z represents:

   A. Sugar
   B. Oxygen
   C. Nitrogen
   D. Water vapor

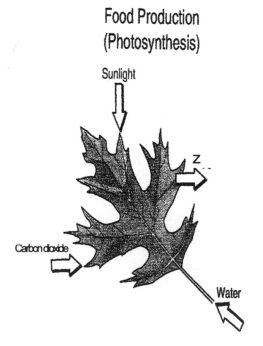

Food Production (Photosynthesis)

Adapted from Texas Assessment of Knowledge and Skills

Question Analysis

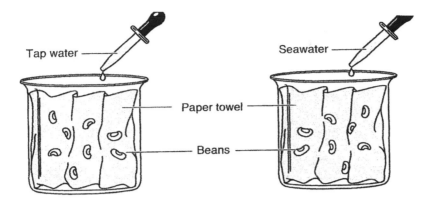

Tap water

Seawater

Paper towel

Beans

3. **Which of these questions can be answered from the results of this experiment?**

    F. Do paper towels help beans to grow?
    G. Can beans grow faster in groups of eight?
    H. Does seawater affect bean growth?
    J. How much water is needed for beans to grow?

---

4. **Jill has a bag with 20 tiles numbered 1 to 20. If she picks out one tile without looking, what is the probability that the number on the tile will be an odd number?**

    A. 1 out of 10
    B. 1 out of 20
    C. 10 out of 10
    D. 10 out of 20

Adapted from Texas Assessment of Knowledge and Skills

Question Analysis

5. A math club decided to buy T-shirts for its members. A clothing company quoted the following prices for the T-shirts:

Math Club T-shirts

Number of T-shirts	Total Cost (dollars)
10	125
15	175
20	225

Which equation best describes the relationship between the total cost, c, and the number of T-shirts, s?

A. c = 12.75s
B. c = 1.75s
C. c = 10s - 25
D. c = 25 + 10s

Adapted from Texas Assessment of Knowledge and Skills

Developing a Rubric

1. Identify 3-5 criteria.

2. Set up a grid with numerical values; 1-4 is usually enough.

3. Identify what would be an excellent piece of work. That becomes a 4.

4. Work backwards. Identify what would be a 3, a 2, and so on. What would be unacceptable? That becomes a 1.

—Ruby Payne

Note: Please see Appendix C for examples of rubrics.

Rubric Guidelines

1. Purpose is to identify desired level of achievement and to set standard.

2. It must be simple and easy to understand. It is appropriate when the individual using it understands it. If a student is to use it, he/she must be able to understand it.

3. Student growth toward desired level of achievement must be clear. The extent to which the student has met the standard must be clear.

4. It can be changed to meet the need.

—Ruby Payne

Note: Please see Appendix C for examples of rubrics.

www.ahaprocess.com

APPENDIX A
MORE ON THE *WHAT*, THE *WHY*, THE *HOW*

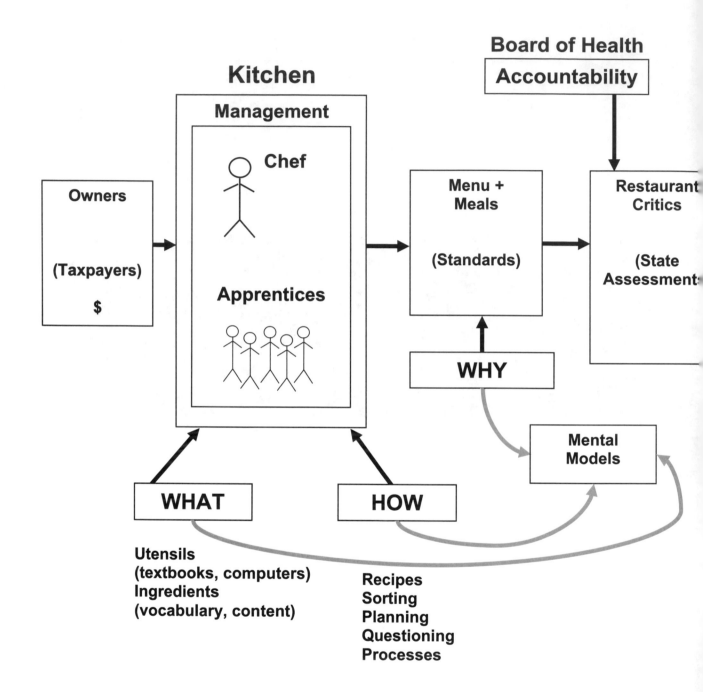

Kitchen

Board of Health

Accountability

Management

Chef

Apprentices

Owners

(Taxpayers)

$

**Menu +
Meals**

(Standards)

**Restaurant
Critics**

**(State
Assessment**

WHY

**Mental
Models**

WHAT

HOW

Utensils
(textbooks, computers)
Ingredients
(vocabulary, content)

Recipes
Sorting
Planning
Questioning
Processes

The Chef Analogy

Ruby K. Payne, Ph.D.

The current educational situation is like a restaurant.

OWNER   KITCHEN   MENU   RESTAURANT   BOARD OF HEALTH
The owner (*taxpayers and legislators*) determines how much money the kitchen has for buying utensils, investing in personnel, purchasing space, etc., and he/she determines what the restaurant meals will be, as well as the purpose of the restaurant.

The kitchen is run by the chef (*teacher*) and has apprentices (*students*).

The meals (*standards*) represent what the kitchen (*classroom*) has to offer to its customers. Each meal is food with high nutritional value and is to represent the best food, presentation, and taste available. No junk food is to be on the menu!

The restaurant is where the public comes to eat. The public includes the critics (*state assessment and accountability*) who put their ratings in the newspaper. The public also includes *parents* who may or may not agree with the critics because their children are the apprentices in the kitchen. The restaurant manager *(administrator)* works to oversee the delivery of the meal to the public.

If the critics (*state assessment*) are unhappy with the restaurant and publish the results in the paper, it creates revenue problems for the owner, which then impacts the kitchen. There is a board of health (*accountability*) that can shut the kitchen down.

The kitchen (*classroom*) is where the key activity occurs. The chef (*teacher*) controls the kitchen (*classroom*) but doesn't control who the apprentices (*students*) are that he/she gets, as *the purpose of the kitchen is to get everyone to cook excellent meals.* Many of the apprentices have never been in a kitchen before. Many don't know the basic vocabulary of the kitchen and don't know sugar from flour.

In this kitchen, the chef (*teacher*) has a physical arrangement and a management system (*classroom management*). The chef has utensils (*computers, textbooks, manipulatives, labs, calculators, equipment*) and ingredients (*vocabulary and content*). The chef has a menu (*lesson plan*) and the apprentices have recipes (*such processes as planning, questioning, sorting, controlling impulsivity, scientific process, writing process, etc.*) that provide a how-to approach to preparing the meal.

So the chef has to pay attention to his/her APPRENTICES and THE WHAT, THE WHY, and THE HOW of his/her kitchen, or the meals will never be prepared.

THE WHAT is the utensils and the ingredients (*materials, content, textbooks, vocabulary*).
THE WHY is the meal (*the standards and their relationship to the purpose of the content*).
THE HOW is the recipes (*student plans*) and the processes (*questioning, sorting, content processes, labeling*) for the apprentices and the menus (*lesson plans*) and management systems (*classroom management and discipline*) for the chef.

There are three pressing problems in the kitchen right now.

First, the chef (*teacher*) doesn't like the meals (*standards*) that he/she is expected to prepare. The chef argues that not everyone likes that food, that the gourmet meals are too much for beginning apprentices to prepare, and that the critics (*state assessments)* and board of health (*accountability*) are totally unfair.

The second pressing problem in the kitchen is the apprentices (*students*). Many of these apprentices have never been in a kitchen. Many don't know the names of the ingredients, much less what a recipe is. Some of the apprentices do know how to cook, but they don't like the meals they are to prepare. Several of the apprentices don't even want to be in a kitchen, so they create difficulties.

The third pressing problem is that many owners (*taxpayers and legislators*) don't understand the kitchen. Some restaurant managers (*administrators*) don't care what happens in the kitchen, so long as there are no visible problems in the restaurant itself. Some restaurant managers are so overwhelmed by the issues in the restaurant they don't even know what's happening in the kitchen.

So … many chefs (*teachers*) are frustrated. <u>And, in desperation, some chefs are only</u> addressing <u>ONE PART of the kitchen.</u> For example, some chefs get no meals prepared because of the difficulties presented by the apprentices. Some chefs go to the owners and restaurant managers and get additional sous-chefs (*more special education and more specialists*) to help them with the apprentices. Some chefs concentrate completely on THE WHAT – the utensils and equipment (*textbooks and materials*) – but don't address THE WHY or THE HOW. They spend hundreds of thousands of dollars on the latest equipment. Some chefs spend all their time on one aspect of the meal – colored frosting on the cake – but don't provide a complete meal because the apprentices like making colored frosting. Some chefs believe that the apprentices should have no recipes (*THE HOW*) because they should have that basic understanding, and it shouldn't have to be articulated. And many chefs don't understand the nutritional value of the meal (*the standards and their relationship to the purpose of the content*) because traditional chef training doesn't provide information on nutritional value. So the chef will substitute lard for butter and cocoa for chocolate. Then the critics complain about the meal.

www.ahaprocess.com

In successful kitchens there's an excellent working relationship between the restaurant manager and the chef. Furthermore, the chef pays close attention to the apprentices and creates mutual respect with the apprentices. The chef always makes certain that THE WHAT, THE WHY, and THE HOW are addressed. The chef uses mental models for THE WHAT, THE WHY, and THE HOW so the apprentices will be able to understand the meal much faster and what needs to be done to prepare it. The chef also knows what the critics want, and the restaurant manager makes certain the restaurant is ready for the critics.

WHAT ARE THE RELATIONSHIPS AMONG STANDARDS, ASSESSMENTS, AND THE STRUCTURE OF CONTENT?

Ruby K. Payne, Ph.D.

To understand the content you are teaching, it is necessary to understand its structure.
In any given area of learning, as that knowledge base develops, it first begins as isolated information. Over time it is linked into chunks of understanding. Those become the basic building blocks, or constructs, of that content. All content has "the WHAT" (the vocabulary), "the WHY" (the relationship of that idea to a greater understanding), and "the HOW" (the abstract processes necessary to use that information in practical reality).

Let's use food as an example. Eons ago the main issue around food was having enough to eat, and our human forebears hunted and gathered. Eventually a knowledge base grew around gathering food, hunting for food, and foods that were poisonous versus ones that were not. Then individuals discovered that some food had medicinal value, so a knowledge base evolved around that as well. As humankind became more agricultural and less nomadic, knowledge bases also developed around planting and harvesting, storing foods, and preparing foods.

Now we have volumes written about the nutritional values of foods, and companies spend millions of dollars on the research and development of new foods. Cookbooks are written around food preparation. We have restaurant guides, elaborate kitchen equipment, many utensils, and so forth. All have evolving knowledge bases. If one were to study food, then there would be separate units on nutrition, preparation, medicinal uses, planting, harvesting, storage, etc.

If a teacher were to test students on such knowledge, one could test by basic units of understanding. But as the students' knowledge base became more sophisticated, the nature of the questions would change. Questions would represent an integration of understandings between and among the units. For example, one might ask a master chef the following question: "How does the time a bunch of bananas is harvested in Brazil impact the making of banana bread from that bunch in Boston?" This kind of question crosses several units of information. It calls for integrated understanding because it requires the person answering the question to not only know the WHAT but also the WHY and the HOW.

Content or subject areas in school are no different. Each subject area has basic units of understanding. These units of understanding build on each other. Traditional teaching has taught each unit of understanding separately.

The standards and assessments that students are now being tested for focus mostly on the WHY and HOW aspects of knowledge bases. This development requires an integrated approach to the WHAT, the WHY, and the HOW. It requires that assessments be largely at the WHY and HOW level.

Therefore, if a teacher doesn't understand the basic organization of the content—its purpose, its structure (organizational constructs), and the basic processes—then the teacher will have trouble sorting what the student does and does not need to know. A great deal of time in many classrooms gets spent on activities that are cute but don't really count for much.

Let's return to food. If you were teaching students to be master chefs, and you spent three weeks on frosting design and color but spent no time on ingredients of cakes or the procedures necessary to bake a cake, the students would never become master chefs. Furthermore, if you couldn't help students identify the critical ingredients in the cake and the role those ingredients play in the final product, again, the students couldn't become master chefs. If the students didn't understand the difference eggs made in the batter, or oil—or the relative merits of shortening versus butter— again, they would be very limited as chefs.

Take algebra as an example. The purpose of algebra is to find the unknown and to use the symbolic and abstract representations of math to solve problems. In the traditional approach, a great deal of algebra instruction is spent on the algorithms (the processes) necessary to do the equations. In other words, a great deal of time is spent on the HOW. Almost no time is spent on the WHY. When very little time is spent on the WHY, the student has great difficulty applying the information to practical situations.

Let's use language arts as another example. One of the main objectives of language arts is to manipulate organizational patterns and words to communicate. A key structure (organizational pattern) is drama. The reason Shakespeare is studied at the high school level is that Shakespeare was a master at that particular structure. I worked with an English teacher who cried after being informed that ninth-graders were not going to do Shakespeare. She didn't understand the purpose of the content and that particular unit. The purpose of drama was to expose students to that particular organizational pattern. Shakespeare was only a tool in that purpose. Shakespeare was not *the* purpose. And if Shakespeare or another drama is taught by simply reading the play, all the teacher did was spend time on the WHAT. If the test assesses only what happened in the play, the student doesn't understand the structure of drama.

On the other hand, the teacher might ask these kinds of questions:
- Why did the author have the character do _____?
- Why did the author need this character to tell this story?
- What was the purpose of the dialogue in this section of the play?
- How could the author have used this character to scare the reader?

In that case the teacher *would* have given the student a WHY and a HOW understanding so that the student could apply the understandings to such practical realities as writing a drama, developing a sophisticated video game, etc.

Let's use beginning reading as a final example. In order to read, one must do two things—decode (this letter goes with this sound) and comprehend (the words can be used to make meaning). The research in kindergarten is that spending time learning the relationship between the *sound* and the letter is a key correlate to learning to read. But if teachers spend most of their time on the *name* of the letter and little time on the *sound* of the letter, then teachers aren't conveying the essence of reading to their students.

Further, to comprehend a story research indicates that a student must understand story structure. To do so, a student must hear or read at least two stories a week. Additionally, the activity that best predicts one's ability to comprehend is the *amount* of reading one does. If a teacher and students spend the majority of time on worksheets and not actually reading, once again the time and emphasis are on the WHAT and not on the WHY and the HOW.

THE LESSON DESIGN

The following lesson design represents the bare bones that must be present in a lesson.

Payne Lesson Design

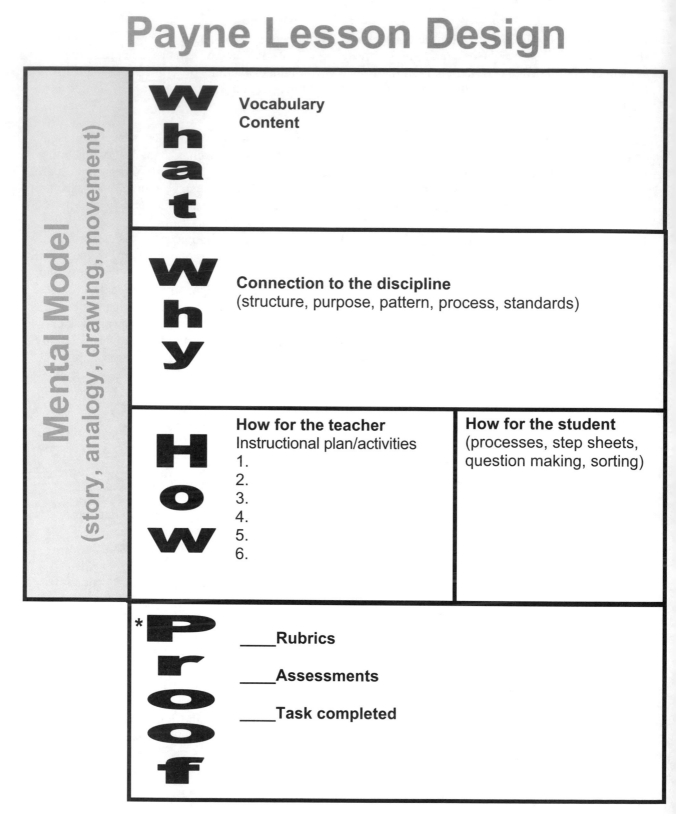

Mental Model
(story, analogy, drawing, movement)

What
Vocabulary
Content

Why
Connection to the discipline
(structure, purpose, pattern, process, standards)

How
How for the teacher
Instructional plan/activities
1.
2.
3.
4.
5.
6.

How for the student
(processes, step sheets, question making, sorting)

*Proof
____Rubrics

____Assessments

____Task completed

* This should be shared with students.

IN CONCLUSION

The current standards and assessments zero in on the WHY (basic structures of the content) and the HOW (basic processes). Because most teachers tend to think in terms of the WHAT (units of instruction), this disparity can be frustrating. But if teachers know the purpose, the structures, the patterns (subsets of the structure), and the processes of their content, it is not so frustrating.

There is a simple rule: IF YOU SPEND MOST OF YOUR TIME ON THE *WHY* AND THE *HOW*, YOU HAVE AUTOMATICALLY TAUGHT THE *WHAT*. You had to teach it because the WHAT is the vocabulary. To teach the HOW and the WHY, you had to use the vocabulary.

Finally, a growing body of research demonstrates that teachers who spend the bulk of their time on the HOW and the WHY rather than on the WHAT have students with much higher achievement.

APPENDIX B
BOARD OF
HEALTH/ACCOUNTABILITY

Improving Test Scores and Student Achievement

Process 1: Identifying Students by Quartile

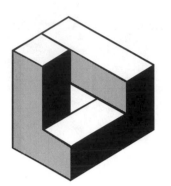

Simple exercise to:
1. Predict assessment rating.
2. Address equity issues—note subgroups not served.
3. Identify specific students to target.
4. Enable timely intervention.

Quartile	Native American	Hispanic	African American	Asian	Caucasian	Low socio-economic status
75-100%						
50-74%						
25-49%						
0-24%						

Tracking student progress by quartile helps measure student growth and determine the amount of probable progress in a given year. It helps us determine how many students, and specifically which students, we need to move.

Prediction guide: To achieve 80% passing on state assessment, 80% of students must score above 50% on normed reference test.

Excerpted from Meeting Standards and Raising Test Scores Training Manual, *Payne & Magee*

Campuswide Interventions That Improve Student Achievement

By Ruby K. Payne, Ph.D.
Founder and President of aha! Process, Inc.

"With simpler models of staff development that are operational and involve 100 percent of the staff, the roller coaster ride that students take through school can be significantly lessened."

Conversation between a principal new to the building and a supervisor:

Supervisor: "That campus cannot be low-performing again. I do not have any extra money to give you. With the Title 1 money you have at your campus, your school will need to find a way to raise your achievement significantly."

Principal (to herself as she walks to the car): "And just how would that happen? I have 1,100 students, 80 percent low income, 12 new teachers, a mobility rate of 40 percent. I know it can be done, but in a year?"

Many of our models for staff development and curriculum development do not address realities pressuring schools today. Some of these realities are:

◆ The critical mass needed to impact student achievement. Example: Ninety percent of teachers are doing a particular intervention or strategy versus 10 percent doing it.

◆ The growing knowledge base required of teachers and administrators. Example: Educators are to know about sexual harassment, inclusion, cooperative learning, reading strategies, ADHD, modifications, gifted/ talented strategies, legal guidelines, ESL, strategies, etc.

◆ The time frames in which student achievement is to occur and be measured. Example: State and norm-referenced tests are designed for annual measures of learning.

◆ The accountability criteria that schools must meet. Example: In Texas, AEIS data and TAAS data are used to determine accreditation status.

◆ The lack of money and time for extensive training for teachers. Example: Most districts and campuses have five days or less of staff development, which limits the length and/or depth of the training.

◆ The increased numbers of students who come from poverty and/or who lack support systems at home.

Example: Educated parents, when the school system does not address their children's needs, tend to provide assistance, pay for a tutor, or request a teacher. In poverty, the student only gets interventions through school.

◆ The increased number of new teachers spurred by the increase in the school-age population. Example: The school-age population in America will increase by 25 percent in the next decade.

Processes and models are available to address these needs. But to do so, an additional model for staff development and curriculum development must be used. This model basically trades in depth learning for critical mass by using a simpler approach. Fullan talks about the importance of critical mass as well as the main criteria teachers use to determine how "user-friendly" the curriculum and training are, i.e., how operational they are. (Fullan, 1991; Fullan, 1996)

In these models, which I have used for several years, the amount of time spent in training is decreased, the model is less complex and totally operational, and 100 percent of the staff is trained. *We still need reflective staff development;* we just need an additional model to help address some of the issues above.

Figure A outlines some of the basic differences.

What does this information mean

in practice? With simpler models that are operational and involve 100 percent of the staff, the roller coaster ride that students take through school can be significantly lessened. One of the reasons that middle-class students do better in school is that their parents intervene to lessen the impact of the roller coaster. (These parents do so by paying for tutoring, requesting teachers and providing assistance and instruction at home.)

As you can see in Figure B, the X represents Johnny and his journey through five years of school. In first grade, he had a wonderful teacher who willingly went to every kind of training available. Johnny had a great year and made the expected progress.

In second grade, his teacher was having many health problems and missed quite a few days of school. In addition, Johnny's parents divorced so he was shuttled between homes. In the second grade, Johnny actually regressed.

In the third grade, he had a beginning teacher. She loved the students but did not have the experience or the guidelines to provide the instruction that the other third-grade teacher did. Most of the educated parents had asked for the other teacher because of her excellent reputation. Johnny made progress.

In the fourth grade, Johnny had a teacher who did not participate in staff development. As far as she was concerned, it was a waste of time. Her students tended to do poorly on the state test, but her husband was on the school board. Once again, given her reputation, the educated parents had requested that their children be placed in the other fourth-grade classroom.

In the fifth grade, it was determined that Johnny was now two-and-a-half grade levels behind and should

How can we address this problem? With systemic interventions that can impact achievement through simple yet effective tools and processes.

Figure A

	Reflective Staff Development	Operational Staff Development
Definition	A process: by which a person examines in-depth his learning on a given subject	A method for immediate implementation across the system to address accountability and student achievement
Purpose	To build in-depth learning and change	To impact the system quickly; to build in connections/linkages across the system
Effects of critical mass	Depends on amount of resources and level of attrition; takes at least four to five years	Affects critical mass almost immediately; can have 80 to 90 percent implementation the first year
Time required	Four to five days per person for initial training	Two hours to one day of training per person
Breadth	Limited	Systemic
Cost analysis	High per-person cost	Low per-person cost
District role	May be contacted or may use district expertise to deliver and provide follow-up	Identify with campuses system needs to be addressed. Works with campuses to reach critical mass. Assists with the operational development of innovation
Follow-up	Provided in small groups or by expert trainer	Provided through accountability measures and the fine tuning from discussions to make innovation more user-friendly
Role of principal	In liaison with training. May provide resources and follow-up opportunities	Assists with the delivery of training. Provides the insistence, support and accountability for innovation.

Figure B

Johnny's progress	Grade 1	Grade 2	Grade 3	Grade 4	Grade 5
Grade 1	X				
Grade 2	X				
Grade 3		X			
Grade 4		X			
Grade 5					

Benjamin Bloom (1976) did extensive research to determine what makes a difference in learning. He identified four factors: 1) the amount of time to learn; 2) the intervention(s) of the teacher; 3) how clear the focus of the instruction is; and 4) what the student came in knowing. As is readily apparent, the control the individual teacher has over these variables is significantly impacted by what is happening at the campus.

When these interventions are addressed at a campus level in a systematic way, more learning occurs.

Systemic interventions that can impact achievement are:

1. *Reasonable expectations.* This is a simpler model of curriculum mapping that addresses the focus of instruction and the amount of time.

2. *Growth assessments.* These are methods for identifying and assessing the growth a student makes on a regular basis.

3. *Benchmarks.* This is a simpler model of three to four indicators by grading period to show whether a student needs an immediate intervention. *It is absolutely crucial for first-grade reading.* Honig (1995) states that a first-grader who is not in the primer by April of the first-grade year generally does not progress beyond the third-grade reading level.

4. *Interventions for the student.* When students are identified through the growth assessments and benchmarks as making inadequate growth, immediate interventions are provided for the student, one of which is allowing more time during the school day.

What follows is a description and example for each of the above. *It is important to note that all of these are working documents of one or two pages so that they can constantly be reassessed.* It is analogous to having a road map: all of the details are not present. However, the lay of the land, the choices of the route and the final destination are clear.

Reasonable expectations

Reasonable expectations identify what is taught and the amount of time devoted to it. This allows a campus to "data mine," i.e., determine the payoff between what actually gets taught, the amount of time given to it and the corresponding test results. For example, if two hours a day are spent on reading but only 15 minutes is devoted to students actually reading, the payoff will be less than if 45 minutes of that time is devoted to students actually reading.

Figure C is the process used. For each subject area, it requires about 30 to 60 minutes of individual time, one to two hours of grade-level time and three hours of total faculty time.

Figure D is an example from Runyan Elementary in Conroe, Texas. The principal is Nancy Harris.

Growth assessments

There are any number of growth assessments available. What makes something a growth assessment is that it identifies movement against a constant set of criteria. What makes a growth assessment different from a test is that the criteria do not change in a growth assessment. Rubrics are one way to measure and identify growth.

Figure E is an example of a reading rubric to measure student growth. It was developed by Sandra Duree, Karen Coffey and me in conjunction with the teachers of Goose Creek ISD. *Becoming a Nation of Readers* identified characteristics of skilled readers, so those characteristics were used to measure growth as a constant over five years. We identified what growth would look like over five years if a student were progressing as a skilled reader.

To develop a growth assessment, a very simple process can be used. Have the teachers in your building (who consistently get the highest achievement, understand the district curriculum and TAAS specs) develop the growth assessment. Keep in mind these guidelines: 1) the purpose is to identify the desired level of

Figure C

Simple Yet Effective Tools and Processes

One of the first pieces of information that a principal and campus need to know is *what is actually being taught.* Here's a simple process to help find this out.

1. If you are on a six-weeks grading period, divide a paper into six equal pieces. If you are on a nine-weeks grading period, divide a paper into four equal pieces. Have each teacher for each subject area write the units or skills that they teach in each grading period. In other words, what do they usually manage to teach to that grade level in that subject area in that amount of time?

2. Have each grade level meet and discuss one subject area at a time. Do all the teachers at a grade level basically have the same expectations for that grade level in terms of content and skills? Have they come to a consensus about the expectation for that grade level?

3. Have the faculty as a group compare the grade levels one through five or six through eight or nine through 12. If Johnny was with the school for five years, what would he have the opportunity to learn? What would he not have had the opportunity to learn? Where are the holes in the opportunities to learn?

4. The faculty then uses this information to identify the strengths and weaknesses in the current educational program. Are some things repeated without benefit to achievement? Are some things not ever taught or so lightly brushed to not be of benefit? What is included that could be traded out for something that has a higher payoff in achievement?

5. When the discussion is over, the one-page sheets are revised and given to the appropriate teachers.

6. Twice a year, the principal meets with grade-level teams, and using these sheets, discusses the progress of the learning, adjustments that need to be made, etc. These become working documents, and because of their simplicity, they can be easily revised.

achievement. 2) the growth assessment needs to be simple and easily understood; and 3) student movement or growth toward the desired level of achievement needs to be clear.

These are the steps to creating a growth assessment:

1. Identify three to five criteria.

2. Set up a grid with numerical values. (One through four is usually enough.)

3. Identify what would be an excellent piece of work or demonstration. That becomes number four.

4. Work backwards. Next identify what would be a three and so on.

When the growth assessment is developed, it needs to go back to the faculty for feedback and refinement. When there is substantial agreement and 80 percent buy-in, the faculty needs to move forward with it.

"Systemic interventions can identify areas where more time needs to be devoted and can address the effectiveness of both the whole and the component parts of the curriculum."

Benchmarks

Figure F is one example.

As you can see from the example, benchmarks are very simple. they identify the critical attributes that students must acquire each six weeks if they are to progress. If the student has not demonstrated these bench-

Figure D

Second Grade Language Arts Curriculum
(70 percent fiction, 30 percent nonfiction)

First six weeks	**Second six weeks**	**Third six weeks**
Reading—60 minutes DEAR—10 minutes Teacher reading to students Reading workshop—50 minutes	*Reading—60 minutes* CEAR—10 minutes Teacher reading to students Reading workshop—50 minutes	*Spelling—60 words total* 10 words per week
Spelling—60 words total 10 words per week	*Spelling—60 words total* 10 words per week	*Writing—45 minutes* Five to seven steps in paragraph, sequential for how-to DOL—15 minutes Writing workshop—30 minutes

Writing—45 minutes
Personal narrative two to three
   sentences same subject
DOL—15 minutes
Writing workshop—30 minutes
	Writing—45 minutes
	Six to seven lines on same
	   subject for how-to
	DOL—15 minutes
	Writing workshop—30 minutes
		*Vocabulary (integrated)—5 words
		   per week*

*Vocabulary (integrated)—5 words
   per week*
	*Vocabulary (integrated)—5 words
	   per week*
		Skills—20 minutes
		Main idea
		Prefix, suffix
		Context clues
		Synonyms, antonyms, homo-
		   phones, homonym
		Comprehension
		Compound words
		Contractions

Skills—20 minutes Choosing a just right book Characters Predicting Distinguishing between fiction and nonfiction	*Skills—20 minutes* Setting Beginning, Middle, End of Story Parts of speech; noun, verb Sequential order Comprehension Compound words Contractions	

Fourth six weeks	**Fifth six weeks**	**Sixth six weeks**
Reading—60 minutes DEAR—15 minutes Teacher reading to students Reading workshop—45 minutes	*Reading—60 minutes* DEAR—15 minutes Teacher reading to students Reading workshop—45 minutes	*Reading—60 minutes* DEAR—15 minutes Teacher reading to students Reading workshop—45 minutes

*Spelling—15 minutes—60 words
   total*
10 words per week
ABC order to second letter
	*Spelling—15 minutes—60 words
	   total*
	10 words per week
	ABC order to third letter
		*Spelling—15 minutes—60 words
		   total*
		10 words per week
		ABC order to third letter

Writing—45 minutes How-to five to seven steps in paragraph form DOL—15 minutes TAAS form Writing workshop—30 minutes	*Writing—45 minutes* Descriptive writing—7 sentences Compare/contrast DOL—15 minutes TAAS form Writing workshop—30 minutes	*Writing—45 minutes* Summary Compare/contrast DOL—15 minutes TAAS form Writing workshop—30 minutes

*Vocabulary (integrated)—5 words
   per week*
	*Vocabulary (integrated)—5 words
	   per week*
		*Vocabulary (integrated)—5 words
		   per week*

Skills—20 minutes
Quotes
Draw conclusions
Main inferences
Adjectives/adverbs
Comprehension
Possessives
Compound words
Contractions
	Skills—20 minutes
	Main idea distinguished from
	   details
	Fact/opinion
	Cause/effect
	Comprehension
	Possessives
	Compound words
	Contractions
		Skills—20 minutes
		Recognize propaganda and point
		   of view
		Comprehension
		Possessives
		Compound words
		Contractions

Figure E

Reading Rubric Grade 1

Student name: _____   School Year: _____

Campus: _____   Grade: _____

	Beginning	**Developing**	**Capable**	**Expert**
Fluency	Decodes words haltingly	Decodes sentences haltingly	Knows vowel teams (ea, ee, oa, etc.)	Decodes polysyllabic words
	Misses key sounds	Knows conditions for long vowels	Identifies common Spelling patterns	Decodes words in context of paragraphs
	Identifies most letter sounds	Identifies blends and consonants	Uses word attack skills to identify new words in the sections	Decodes words accurately and automatically
	Identifies short vowels	Decodes diagraphs and "r" control vowels (or, ar, er, etc.)	Reads sentences in a meaningful sequence	Reads paragraphs in a meaningful sequence
	Says/recognizes individual words	Reads at rate that doesn't interfere with meaning	Reads with expression	Reads with expression, fluency, appropriate tone and pronunciation
Constructive	Predictions are incomplete, partial and unrelated	Predicts what might happen next	Predicts story based upon pictures and other clues	Can predict possible endings to story with some accuracy
	Predictions indicate no or inappropriate prior knowledge	Makes minimal links to personal experience/ prior knowledge	Relates story to personal experience/ prior knowledge	Can compare/contrast story with personal experience
Motivated	Does not read independently	Reads when parent or teacher requests	Will read for a specific purpose	Initiates reading on own
	Concentrates on decoding	Eager to use the acquired skills (words and phrases)	Uses new skills frequently in self-selected reading	Reads for pleasure
Strategic	Does not self-correct	Recognizes mistakes but has difficulty in self-correcting	Has strategies for self-correction (reread, read ahead, ask a question, etc.)	Analyzes self-correction strategies for the best strategy
	Uncertain as to how parts of a story fit together	Can identify characters and setting in a story	Can identify characters, setting and events of a story	Can talk about story in terms of problem and/or goal
Process	Cannot tell what has been read	Does not sort important from unimportant	What is important and unimportant can be determined with assistance	Organizes reading by sorting important from unimportant

marks, then immediate additional interventions must begin.

How does one get benchmarks? Once again, identify the experienced educators who always have high student achievement. Ask them how they know a student will have trouble. They already know the criteria. And by putting it in writing and having a common understanding, teachers, particularly those who are new to teaching or who are not as experienced, can more readily make interventions and address student progress. It then needs to go back to the grade level for their feedback and changes.

Interventions for Students

The issue here is that the intervention be timely and occur at a classroom and a campus level (see Figure G). One other point is simply that for optimal learning, the student needs to stay with the regular instruction, in as much as possible, to have the opportunity to learn what the other students are learning. Additional time for learning must be found (for example, using social studies time to teach nonfiction reading).

Conclusion

What these systemic interventions allow a campus to do is to address the four variables in learning: 1) the amount of time to learn; 2) the intervention(s) of the teacher; 3) how clear the focus of the instruction is; and 4) what the student came in knowing.

It allows the faculty to address the amount of time, the interventions, the clarity of the instructional focus, and what the student had the opportunity to come in knowing. Right now, because of the depth and breadth of most curriculum guides, it is difficult to know that the students actually had the opportunity to learn. By having these systemic items in place, the faculty discussion can truly be data driven; it allows the faculty to talk

about student achievement in relationship to the total curriculum.

The discussion can focus on program strengths and weaknesses. It can identify areas where more time needs to be devoted and can address

the effectiveness of both the whole and the component parts of the curriculum. It allows a faculty to determine staff development that will address student needs, and it provides one more tool for analyzing TAAS data.

Figure F

Benchmarks for fourth-grade language arts

If a student cannot do the following, then immediate interventions need to be used.

First six weeks
- Edit fragments and run-ons in own writing
- Identify and define figurative and literal meaning
- Write an elaborated, organized descriptive paper
- Be able to choose just right books

Second six weeks
- Identify story structure orally and in written form
- Write an organized, elaborated expressive narrative
- Identify correct subject/verb agreement and use in everyday writing

Third six weeks
- Read a passage and use context clues to decode unknown words
- Read a passage and recall facts and details orally and in writing
- Read a story or paragraph and sequence major events
- Write an organized, elaborated how-to

Fourth six weeks
- Read a passage and identify main idea, orally and in written summary
- Read a passage and paraphrase orally and in writing
- Write an organized, elaborated classificatory paper
- Read a passage and identify the best summary
- Write a three to four sentence paragraph

Fifth six weeks
- Use graphic sources to answer questions
- Read passage and predict outcomes and draw conclusions
- Distinguish between fact and nonfact; between stated and nonstated opinion
- After reading a passage, be able to tell cause of an event or effect of an action
- Write an organized, elaborative persuasive paper

Sixth six weeks
- Write an assessment of chosen portfolio pieces
- Assemble/share a reading and writing portfolio

Figure G

Campus Interventions

Curriculum linkages across and within grade levels

Assess time allocation by subject, by activity, and by student

Staff agreement on common language and processes for problem solving, etc.

Identify reasonable expectations and benchmarks

Work with master schedule to identify additional time blocks for interventions

Classroom Interventions
(Just a few of many possible)

Goal setting/controlling impulsivity activities

Teaching procedures

Having students write multiple choice questions

Using music to put learning into long-term memory

Increasing the amount of time the student actually reads and writes

Activities that use figural, kinesthetic and symbolic approaches to learning.

Currently, many campuses address the best objective they were low in the year before, only to fall in other objectives the next year. It allows a new teacher to have a much better sense of expectations. Parents have a much better sense of the learning opportunities students will have.

It provides a tool for principals to dialogue with teachers about learning. But more importantly, it allows the campus to identify before the damage is great the students who are not making sufficient progress and to make that intervention immediately, as opposed to one or two years down the road.

This is the process I used as a principal. Our math scores made significant improvement within two years. I have used it at the secondary level in language arts with excellent results as well.

These simple models and processes give us the tools to talk about what we are doing and to minimize the roller coaster ride for students.

References

Becoming a Nation of Readers. 1984. Center for Study of Reading. University of Illinois. Champagne, Illinois.

Bloom, Benjamin. 1976. *Human Characteristics and School Learning.* McGraw-Hill. New York, New York.

Fullan, Michael G. 1996. Turning Systemic Thinking on Its Head. *Phi Delta Kappan.* February, 1996, pp. 420-423.

Fullan, Michael G. 1996. *The New Meaning of Educational Change.* Teachers College Press. Columbia University. New York, New York.

Previously printed in *Instructional Leader* magazine.

Editors note: Dr. Payne has produced a systemic "how-to approach" to raising student achievement in a course, *Meeting Standards and Raising Test Scores – When You Don't Have Much Time or Money,* consisting of four videos and a training manual. The video course, or a one-day workshop is available on her website, www.ahaprocess.com. Also opt-in to **aha!**'s e-mail newslist for the latest poverty and income statistics [free] and other updates.

Ruby K. Payne, Ph.D., founder and president of **aha!** Process, Inc. (1994), with more than 30 years experience as a professional educator, has been sharing her insights about the impact of poverty – and how to help educators and other professionals work effectively with individuals from poverty – in more than a thousand workshop settings through North America, Canada, and Australia.

Her seminal work, *A Framework for Understanding Poverty,* teaches the hidden rules of economic class and spreads the message that, despite the obstacles poverty can create in all types of interaction, there are specific strategies for overcoming them.

Since publishing *Framework* in 1995, Dr. Payne also has written or co-authored nearly a dozen books surrounding these issues in such areas as education, social services, the workplace, faith communities and leadership. More information can be found on her website, www.ahaprocess.com.

aha! Process, Inc.
(800) 424-9484
(281) 426-5300
fax: (281) 426-5600
www.ahaprocess.com

APPENDIX C
PURPOSE/STRUCTURE/PATTERNS IN DISCIPLINES

Purpose/Structure/Patterns in Disciplines

Just as a blueprint is used to represent a house, so subject matter has blueprints or mental models, i.e., ways in which the information is coded and structured.

The mental models of a subject area come from three sources: the purpose, the pattern, and the structure of the information. These three elements determine the units of study—namely, how the curriculum gets organized. Processes are developed as a way to deal with the purposes, the patterns, and the structures.

CONTENT	PURPOSE
Language Arts	Using structure and language to communicate
Math	Assigning order and value to the universe
Biology	Identifying living systems and relationships within and among those systems
Chemistry	Bonding
Algebra	Solving for the unknown through functions
Geometry	Using logic to order and assign values to form and space
Physics	Using matter and energy through math applications
Social Studies	Understanding ways people interact and live over time
Earth Science	Identifying and predicting physical phenomena

How a discipline translates from the sensory to the abstract representations (mental models) of its content:

STRUCTURE OF THE DISCIPLINE

PURPOSE	
STRUCTURE	
PATTERNS	

Those translate into:

UNITS	STANDARDS	MENTAL MODELS	PROCESSES (INPUT STRATEGIES)

Example: Elementary Reading

PURPOSE	To making meaning from written symbols
STRUCTURES *	Sounds Written symbols (letters) Structures of text Structures of words Structures of sentences Word meaning
PATTERNS	Short and long vowels, diphthongs, etc. Root words, prefixes, suffixes Part to whole of sounds, words, sentences, text Part to whole of text (sentences, paragraphs, etc.) Connotation, denotation, contextual clues Relationships between/among letters and sounds Reading aloud (patterns of voice, speed, intonation, etc.) Types of text (fiction, nonfiction, etc.) Summarization and sorting of important from unimportant Patterns in predicting

* The current terminology (because of the Reading First grant) is phonemic awareness, phonics, vocabulary, fluency, and comprehension.

These translate into:

UNITS	STANDARDS	MENTAL MODELS	PROCESSES (INPUT STRATEGIES)
fluency	Student will decode at a rate that will not interfere with meaning	Tucker Signing Strategies	Part to whole

The STANDARD is then assessed through a rubric.

Reading Rubric, Grade 1

	Beginning	Developing	Capable	Expert
Fluent	Decodes words haltingly	Decodes sentences haltingly	Knows vowel teams (ea, ee, oa, etc.)	Decodes polysyllabic words
	Misses key sounds	Knows conditions for long vowels (vowel at end of syllable, e.g., me, he)	Identifies common spelling patterns	Decodes words in context of paragraph
	Identifies most letter sounds	Identifies blends and consonants	Uses word-attack skills to identify new words	Decodes words accurately and automatically
	Identifies short vowels	Decodes digraphs and r-controlled vowels (or, ar, er, etc.)	Reads sentences in meaningful sequence	Reads paragraphs in meaningful sequence
	Says/recognizes individual words	Reads at rate that does not interfere with meaning	Reads with expression	Reads with expression, fluency, and appropriate tone and pronunciation
Constructive	Predictions are incomplete, partial, and unrelated	Predicts what might happen next	Predicts story based upon pictures and other clues	Can predict possible endings to story with some accuracy
	Predictions indicate no or inappropriate prior knowledge	Makes minimal links to personal experience/prior knowledge	Relates story to personal experience/prior knowledge	Can compare/contrast story with personal experience
Motivated	Does not read independently	Reads when teacher or parent requests	Will read for specific purpose	Self-initiates reading
	Concentrates on decoding	Is eager to utilize acquired skills (words and phrases)	Uses new skills frequently in self-selected reading	Reads for pleasure

Reading Rubric, Grade 1 (continued)

	Beginning	Developing	Capable	Expert
Strategic	Does not self-correct	Recognizes mistakes but has difficulty in self-correcting	Has strategies for self-correction (rereads, reads ahead, asks questions, etc.)	Analyzes self-correction strategies to find best strategy
	Is uncertain as to how parts of story fit together	Can identify characters and setting in story	Can identify characters, settings, and events of story	Can talk about story in terms of problem and/or goal
Process	Cannot tell what has been read	Does not sort important from unimportant	Can determine with assistance what is important and unimportant	Organizes reading by sorting important from unimportant

For example, let's use secondary language arts as an example.

STRUCTURE OF THE DISCIPLINE—LANGUAGE ARTS

PURPOSE	To use structure and language to communicate
STRUCTURES	Literary genres (poetry, drama, fiction, nonfiction, etc.) Syntax of language (grammar) Written structures (persuasive, narrative, etc.) Phonemic structures of language (decoding) Word meaning (vocabulary) Written conventions of language (punctuation, spelling) Oral structures of language (speechmaking, dialogue) Structures of media (advertising, filmmaking, etc.)
PATTERNS (partial listing)	Literary structural patterns (characterization, story structure, point of view, etc.) Literary word patterns (rhythm, alliteration, etc.) Grammatical patterns (adverbial phrases, clauses, etc.) Logic and proof in written and oral persuasion Development of thesis and patterns of written text Patterns in the use of conventions, spelling, etc. Word-meaning patterns (root words, suffixes, verb tenses, etc.) Patterns in decoding (blends, diphthongs, short and long vowels, etc.) Patterns in spelling Common advertising appeals

Those translate into (examples):

UNITS	STANDARDS	MENTAL MODELS	PROCESSES (INPUT STRATEGIES)
Short stories	Students will be able to identify point of view of author.	Drawings of common types of story structures.	Students can sort important from unimportant against criteria and therefore determine author's purpose.

The STANDARD is then assessed with rubrics.

Rubric for Analysis of Point of View
(highlight the indicators that apply to the story)

SELECTED STORY	USE OF DIALOGUE	USE OF STORY STRUCTURE	USE OF WORD CHOICE	USE OF CHARACTER DEVELOPMENT	PLOT OR CHARACTER OMISSIONS	TELLER
Story A	Dialogue used to develop plot Dialogue used to develop character (i.e., indicate intelligence) Dialogue used to convey feelings	Story starts in middle and uses flashbacks Story uses chronological order (in time) Story is story within story Story is stream of consciousness Episodic story structure (series of situations involving one character)	Words often used to convey feelings Words used to convey action Words used to describe Word choice is angry, happy, bitter, ____ Use of pronouns (I, we, she)	Main character developed through interactions with other characters Main character developed through dialogue about main character Main character developed through situations Main character developed through conflicts Main character developed through absence	What is *not* in dialogue about main character Key scenes that are only referenced or omitted Accuracy of character comments about self or others Story told by only one person	Told in third person Told in first person Told through dreams Told as retelling Told in present tense Told in past tense
Story B	Dialogue used to develop plot Dialogue used to develop character (i.e., indicate intelligence) Dialogue used to convey feelings	Story starts in middle and uses flashbacks Story uses chronological order (in time) Story is story within story Story is stream of consciousness Episodic story structure (series of situations involving one character)	Words often used to convey feelings Words used to convey action Words used to describe Word choice is angry, happy, bitter, ____ Use of pronouns (I, we, she)	Main character developed through interactions with other characters Main character developed through dialogue about main character Main character developed through situations Main character developed through conflicts Main character developed through absence	What is *not* in dialogue about main character Key scenes that are only referenced or omitted Accuracy of character comments about self or others Story told by only one person	Told in third person Told in first person Told through dreams Told as retelling Told in present tense Told in past tense

STRUCTURE OF THE DISCIPLINE—MATHEMATICS

PURPOSE	Assign order and value to universe
STRUCTURES	Numbers Space Time
PATTERNS (partial listing)	Fractions (part to whole of space) Decimals (part to whole of numbers) Measurement (assign order and value to space and time) Integers Place value
PROCESSES	Problem solving—multiplication, addition, subtraction, division

STRUCTURE OF THE DISCIPLINE—SCIENCE

PURPOSE	Order, explain, and classify living and non-living environment
STRUCTURES	Humans Animals Plants Matter Energy Waves Systems Time Space
PATTERNS (partial listing)	Replication Birth Death Interdependence Measurement Growth Mobility/movement Developmental stages Relationships between and among systems and entities Relationships between and among time and space Classification
PROCESSES	Scientific process (hypothesis, gathering proof, etc.)

STRUCTURE OF THE DISCIPLINE—SOCIAL STUDIES

PURPOSE	Ways human beings live and interact over time
STRUCTURES	Chronological (sequentially over time) Topical (wars, economics, etc.) Descriptive (story format)
PATTERNS (partial listing)	Military Geographic Mobility/movement Political Governments Familial Religious Arts Cultural Rise and fall of civilizations Leadership

STRUCTURE OF THE DISCIPLINE—ATHLETICS

PURPOSE	To compete
STRUCTURES	Physical attributes of players Equipment Rules of the game Playing field
PATTERNS (partial listing)	Drills Plays Categories of players Strategies Skill acquisition Practice
PROCESS	Repetition

STRUCTURE OF THE DISCIPLINE—MUSIC

PURPOSE	To use sounds and instruments to make meaning
STRUCTURES	Voice Instruments Sounds (keys, notes, etc.) Time Written notations
PATTERNS	Groups of instruments Patterns of time (rhythm, beat, half notes, etc.) Patterns of sounds (keys, notes, sharps, flats, etc.) Patterns in notations Kinds of voices (bass, tenor, etc.) Voice ranges Voice quality Terminology in written notation Interpretation Group patterns (orchestra, band, ensemble, choir, etc.)

RUBRIC TO MEASURE A SKILLED MUSICIAN (in band and orchestra)

CRITERIA	1	2	3	4
ACCURACY	Not in time Several wrong notes Wrong key	Mostly in correct time Misses notes Key is correct Fingerings are off	In correct time Mostly uses correct fingerings Notes are correct	Timing is virtually always correct Fingerings are correct Notes are virtually always correct
ARTICULATION	No variation in tempo Markings not observed No contrast in sound	Some variation in tempo but not correct Some contrast but incorrect for piece Random use of markings	Tempo mostly correct Mostly correct use of markings Dynamic contrast thin but correct	Markings are virtually always observed and followed Wide range of dynamic contrast Tempo is correct
SOUND QUALITY	Thin timbre High and low notes off Too loud or too soft for note or section Unpleasant to ear	Timbre for most notes is fuller All difficult notes have some timbre Use of sound markings is random	Timbre is mostly full Sound markings are used but not advantageously	Timbre is full Sound markings are correctly interpreted and followed
INTERPRETATION	No meaning assigned to piece No understanding of intent or purpose of composer	Playing indicates emotion but little understanding of meaning Understands that piece has climax but does not know where it is	Playing mostly conveys meaning and always conveys emotion Understands role of climax Can talk about intent and purpose	Playing conveys meaning and emotion Climax can be identified Plays truly to intent and purpose
ENSEMBLE CONTRIBUTION	Does not pay attention to conductor Listens only to his/her playing Too loud/too soft for group	Periodically pays attention to conductor Is mostly in balance with group Listens to his /her section Little understanding of his/her contribution to melody	Mostly follows conductor's interpretations In balance with group Mostly listens to piece as whole Can verbally articulate contribution to melody but does not always reflect that in his/her playing	Follows conductor's interpretation In balance with group Listens to piece as whole Understands his/her contribution to melody

Appendix D
HOW TO USE THE WORKBOOK PAGES

Learning Structures:
the *What*, the *Why*, the *How*
Workbook Activity Directions

MODULE 8: Learning Structures: the *What*, the *Why*, the *How*

Chef Analogy (page 2)

- The Chef Analogy drawing is a mental model for this book and is explained in depth in the article "The Chef Analogy" by Dr. Ruby K. Payne in Appendix A. The Chef Analogy drawing is blank so that participants can add the information themselves as it is discussed.

Processing (page 3)

- This diagram shows what separates the body, the mind, the ability to think, and the ability to analyze. What separates the body from the mind are emotions; what separates the mind from metacognition (ability to think) are mental models or abstract representations; what separates metacognition (ability to think) from epistemic cognition is the ability to analyze the framework or the theoretical structure of one's thinking.

- If you are a welder, at the body level you weld. This level involves the senses— taste, touch, etc., and the person acts on his/her feelings. At the next level, the mind, you can talk about welding. You feel the feeling. The abstract representative systems involved include associativity like intuition and emotions. The next level is metacognition, the ability to think about thinking. At this level you weld against a blueprint. At this level there is also something that represents the feeling. Included at this level are mental models, which help translate from the sensory to the abstract. At the epistemic cognition level, you can assess blueprints for structural strength. Systems and theory are involved.

Payne Lesson Design (page 4)

- The Payne Lesson Design represents the "bare bones" that must be present in a lesson and is discussed in depth in the article "What Are the Relationships Among Standards, Assessments, and the Structure of Content?" by Ruby Payne in Appendix A.

MODULE 9: Mental Models Help Understand the *Why* and Translate the Concrete to the Abstract

Concrete/Abstract (page 8)

- This diagram shows that to translate the concrete to the abstract the mind needs to hold the information in a mental model. A mental model can be a two-dimensional visual representation, a story, a metaphor, or an analogy.

Five Generic Mental Models (page 9)

- This chart shows the five generic mental models for dealing with school and work— and what they provide for the student.

Sketching Vocabulary: Word/Picture (page 10)

- This activity has the student write a word in the first column, then draw a picture (a visual representation of the word) in the second column. If the student cannot draw a visual representation of the word, he/she probably does not know the word. One of the fastest ways to teach vocabulary in any subject is to have students sketch. If they cannot sketch the word, they do not know it.

Examples of Sketching (page 11)

- These are student examples of sketching activities using certain math terms: isosceles triangle, scalene triangle, rhombus, and vertices.

Mental Model for Formal Register—Written Expression (page 12)

- This mental model is for formal register. A sentence starts with a capital letter and ends with a punctuation mark. It has a subject and a verb. A straight line is the subject, and a wavy line is the verb. A rectangle describes the subject, and a triangle expands the verb. A triangle answers one of four questions: how, when, where, or why.

Mental Model for Space (page 13)

- Mental model for space: This is one way in which we diagnose, ascertain, and teach space.

- Stand up and put the end of your pencil or pen on the end of your nose like this. Face me. The tip of your pencil is the tip of the arrow. This dot is your arm. Now the question is as follows: To which side of the tip of the arrow is the dot? And the answer to your first box (upper-left-hand corner) is <u>left</u>.

- This is called <u>directionality</u>. If you cannot do this, you have serious problems in math and problems on IQ tests.

- This is exactly how we teach directionality and get it inside students' heads. We say to them, "You know, inside your head you're holding information, and when your eyes go up, it helps you get the pictures that you have inside your head and put them in there … We are going to do this inside your head—get the picture in here."

- Students cannot be neat unless you give them a representational system to carry in their heads. As an example help students develop a map of their desk. This is an <u>abstract representation</u>, students cannot find things without it.

Mental Model for Social Studies (page 14)

- The interior box is the smallest component of government. As the boxes increase in size, they illustrate the layers, connections, and components of government.

Mental Model for Social Studies (blank) (page 15)

- On the blank model provided have students color each box a different color. Students replicate the pattern moving from the center outward. Students should note specific examples within each box related to the area or type of government under investigation.

Mental Model for Part to Whole (page 16)

- Have students take a manila folder and glue six envelopes onto the inside of it with the flaps on the outside. This helps them visually see *part to whole*, especially when they have to divide a report into parts. When you first teach this you may need to give them some of the groupings, but after two or three times they can figure it out.

Mental Models in Math for Multiplication of Positive and Negative Numbers
(page 17)

- With this activity you are teaching pattern recognition. Positive in the first column is the good guy. Minus is a bad guy. Positive in the second column means the good guys are coming to town. Negative means they're leaving town. The third column is what you get. Positive in the third column means good; negative means bad. Good guys are coming to town: good or bad? Good. So you multiply a positive times a positive and you get a positive. Good guys are leaving town: good or bad? Bad. You don't want them leaving. A positive times a negative is a negative. Bad guys are coming to town: good or bad? Bad. You don't want them coming. Bad guys are leaving town: good or bad? Good.

Mental Models for Analogies (page 18)

- What you want the students to look at in this activity involves relationships. In the first box is a circle with half of it shaded. In the next-to-last box (top row) is a square that is half shaded. What do you want the students to draw in the last box? A square that is shaded on the top half. Then have them make the visual analogy using relationships with the last line.

Mental Model of the Pythagorean Theorem (page 19)

Pythagorean Theorem

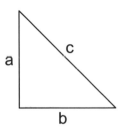

- The Pythagorean Theorem is $a^2 + b^2 = c^2$. This diagram represents the geometric proof of the formula.

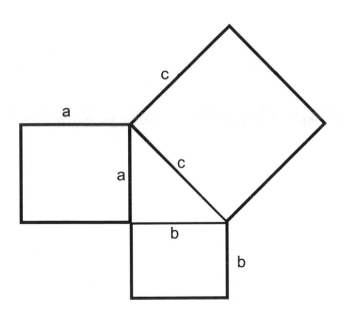

- What the theorem is stating is that if you square the length of side a (represented by the square with side lengths of a) and square the length of side b (represented by the square with side lengths of b), the combined area of the two squares will equal the area of square of side c (represented by the square with side lengths of c).

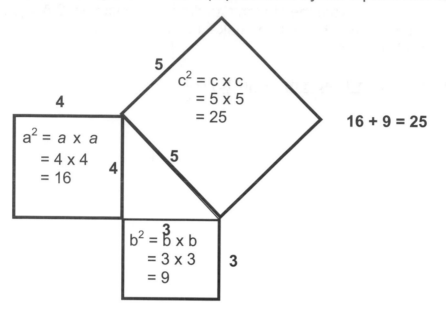

- Therefore, the length of each side of the right triangle is the square root of the area of that side squared.

Mental Model for Time: Planning Backwards (page 21)

- When you have students who don't have a mental model for time, they cannot sequence, plan, follow directions, or match abstract time and tasks. A technique for helping students deal with time is called planning backwards. You can use this sample sheet to develop your own "planning backwards" activity by starting with the last activity first and moving backwards. For instance, go to the last box—the day the project is due. Below the box have the students make a list of tasks they must do to finish the assignment. Then ask the students, "What do you have to do the day it is due?" Then, "What do you have to do the day before it is due?" and so forth. Eventually you help the class pace the activities in such a way that the entire project can be done.

Term Paper Planning (page 22)

- This is an example of a "planning backwards" sheet to use with students who are writing a term paper.

Plan, Do, Review (page 23)

- This is another activity sheet that you can use with students to help them with sequencing, planning, following directions, and matching abstract time and tasks.

At the beginning of class they answer the question, "What is your plan for today?" They then write the order in which they are going to do the tasks. At the end of class, they answer this question: "Did you do your plan? Why or why not?" For the younger children, the plans can be in the form of drawn pictures. Make photocopies of this form and help them complete the sheet.

Step Sheet (page 24)

- This activity is called a step sheet, a tool that helps students who ask what they should do even before you finish the directions for an assignment. Step sheets provide procedural information for academic tasks. If students cannot plan, they often do not have procedural self-talk. They tend to do the first few steps, then quit. A step sheet helps them successfully do the task every time.

English III—Making the Grade (page 25)

- At the beginning of the grading period, the teacher asks students to answer questions about the kinds of grades they want. Then each Friday the teacher gives 15 minutes for the students to record their grades from the week, calculate their averages, and identify what they must do to maintain or bring up their grades.

Spring Semester (page 26)

- This form is for students to use. It contains the percentage that daily work, quizzes, and tests count toward their quarterly grade. There is a place for them to record their actual grades.

MODULE 10: Strategies for Teaching the *What*

Vocabulary Strategies (pages 29-36)

- All instructions for completing these activities are included on the activity pages themselves.

Vocabulary Word Map (page 37)

- Have the students write a vocabulary word in the box in the middle of the page under vocabulary word. Then have the students write the definition or synonym for the word in the box for definition or synonym. Have the student then write on the line an antonym for the word. Next the students should be able to use the word in a sentence. Finally, have the students sketch a mental model for the word. If the word is *love*, they might draw a heart. If the word is *religion*, they might draw a cross or a church.

MODULE 11: Strategies for Teaching the *How*

Cognitive Strategies (page 41)

- Reuven Feuerstein talks a lot about input strategies and gathering data. Not only do students have to gather data, they also have to use the data and communicate the data. Our current system of schooling is based on the concept that we start teaching at elaboration. We talk about that ready-to-learn "stuff." What we mean is that the child has these input strategies because the parent will give the child these. When parents don't give such strategies by third grade, we put the child in special education.

Problem-Solving Process (page 43)

- Read the problem.
- Reread the problem and the question.
- Mark the information.
- Choose an appropriate strategy.
- Solve.
- Is the question answered?

Plan and Label in Math (page 44)

- This is an example of *plan and label* as it pertains to division. Each of the six steps is an example of the *plan and labels* the students must be able to identify and follow to work through the steps of division.

  One, two, and three (1-3) are the parts of the equation that the students should be able to identify and label. Four, five, and six (4-6) are the steps or the plan that the students need to follow to be able to work the division problem. These steps identify the questions/plan that the students must be able to answer/follow to solve the division equation.

Plan and Label: Identifying Characteristics (page 45)

- Plan and Label for Academic Tasks: Look at the sample. In each of the two frames, make a new drawing using the changes indicated.

Plan and Label Space (page 46)

- The map shown represents the shape of the contiguous United States. This map is solid and focuses on the outline, but other maps could be used to illustrate states and physical features.

www.ahaprocess.com

- Have students select a box from the top grid and count to locate the exact box in the grid below. Students should then replicate the boundary line in the new box, ultimately connecting the boundary line all the way around the map.

Plan and Label in Science (page 47)

- This is a process/concept chart. The student tells what is done and explains how. Step 1: The vinegar is poured into a dish. Why? … Because it provides electrons and ions. Step 2: Pieces of cloth are dipped into vinegar. Why? ... Because it provides a conductor and insulator. Step 3: The cloth is placed between pieces of copper and zinc. Why? ... Because they give and take electrons. Step 4: There are four stacks of cloth, zinc, and copper. Why do we need to stack four?... Because it makes a current. Step 5: Aluminum foil connects the top and bottom of the stack. Why? … Because it makes a circuit. Step 6: A light is placed at the top. Why? … To close the circuit. Basically, you can use this in any lab activity. The students are given the steps, but they have to explain why. The next step up would be to have the students create or plan their own steps and explain why. This is a higher level of inquiry, and the plan is on paper before they perform the experiment. They have to "think" through before they act. This is a great way to have students plan … explaining not only the process but the concept behind the process.

Reading Strategies (pages 48-50)

- Most state assessments have gone to a high percentage of the text being nonfiction. Inside your head you sort nonfiction differently than fiction. Use these reading strategies with the article "The Little Armored One" and with the questions that follow the article.

Classificatory Writing (page 51)

- This activity shows the students what each paragraph contains and how many paragraphs a piece of classificatory writing should have. This is another form of a step sheet because it provides procedural information for an academic task.

Identifying Characteristics (page 54)

- Using the column on the left, identify how the examples to the right are alike and different from the column on the left. Circle the words that indicate the way(s) in which the examples to the right are the same.

Identifying Characteristics: Words—Alike and Different (page 55)

- In the first column write what the words have in common. In the second column write how the words are different.

Sorting by Criteria and Patterns: Cartoon Chapter (page 56)

- Have students use this activity to draw their own cartoon characters or have them cut out cartoon characters they find in the newspaper. Have the students sort them using criteria and patterns that they develop through their drawings or through the characters they choose to cut out and paste in the squares.

Five Models to Use for Sorting (page 57)

- Students will get much higher comprehension if they use one of the five techniques for sorting. In nonfiction there are five kinds of text. Each icon represents the five kinds of text and gives students a quick memory tool.

Sorting Model #1: Descriptive/Topical (page 58)

- The hand is topical or descriptive. Use each finger to sort topics or descriptive details.

Sorting Model #2: Sequence/How-to (page 59)

- Use the car as a model to sort and remember. For example, in a piece of fiction there are characters, the beginning, the middle, the end, the episode, the problem, the goal, and the setting.

Sorting Model #3: Story Structure (page 60)

- Label sequential steps on a ladder.

Sorting Model #4: Compare/Contrast, Advantages/Disadvantages, Cause/Effect (page 61)

- Use the two sides of the T-shape to compare and contrast.

Sorting Model #5: Persuasive Reasons (page 62)

- If you use a hamburger, the top bun represents the person's position. Each layer in the sandwich is a piece of supporting evidence. The bottom bun is the conclusion.

Writing Multiple-Choice Questions (page 64)

- If twice a week, instead of having students answer the questions at the end of the chapter you have them *write* the questions, their test scores will "shoot up." Use this form to have students develop their own multiple choice questions. They must follow the three rules listed at the bottom of the form.

Math Questions (page 65)

- In writing math questions, you want to make sure in your stems that you have the terminology that is being used.

- Errors students might make to come up with an answer are as follows:
  - Added all the numbers together
  - Used the wrong operation
  - Missed information

- Have students identify why the wrong answer is wrong.

Reading-Objective Question Stems (page 66)

- Test makers call the question part the stem; the answer choices are called the distractors.

- Put students in pairs and give them one of these pages and stems to use to write questions.

Science Question Stems (Ninth Grade) (page 67)
Question Stems (Fifth- and Ninth-Grade Reading) (page 68)

- Test makers call the question part the stem; the answer choices are called the distracters. Put students in pairs and give them one of these pages of stems. Then have students use these question stems to develop their own questions.

- Analyze questions from your state assessment and compile stems appropriate to it.

MODULE 12: Putting It All Together: Lesson Design

Payne Lesson Design (page 72)
Payne Lesson Design (page 73)

- The first Payne Lesson Design represents the "bare bones" that must be present in a lesson and is discussed in depth in Module 8 in the article "What Are the Relationships Among Standards, Assessments, and the Structure of Content?" by Ruby Payne. Use the article titled "Diet During Pregnancy Could Have Effects That Last to Adulthood" to complete the Lesson Plan in detail.

- The second Payne Lesson Design shows some of what should be completed using the chart titled "Epigenetics: Patterns of Gene Silencing and Activation" on page 74.

MODULE 13: Assessment

Question Analysis Form (page 77)

- Use this form to analyze the questions the students develop. Have them use the form to evaluate each other's questions as they work in pairs and in groups.

Question Analysis (pages 78-80)

- These are sample test questions adapted from the Texas state assessment test. Analyze them to see if they are good questions and if you can ascertain the correct answers to the questions. Obtain sample test questions from your own state assessment tests and use them as models for writing test questions for your own students—and for having them write their own test questions.

- Use these activity pages to help your students develop their cognitive capacity (the ability to ask questions). Question making is developmental, but if by the end of second grade students still cannot formulate questions, it will probably impact their reading. Annemarie Palincsar notes that if students can ask questions syntactically, their reading is much better.

Developing a Rubric (page 81)
Rubric Guidelines (page 82)

- Use these two pages to develop rubrics for not only the classes you teach but also for individual assignments. Give students the rubric so that they know the criteria for their work. (See Appendix A for examples of rubrics.)

APPENDIX A
More on the *What*, the *Why*, the *How*

- Included in this appendix are the completed Chef Analogy diagram; the article "The Chef Analogy" by Ruby K. Payne, Ph.D.; and the article "What Are the Relationships among Standards, Assessments, and the Structure of Content?" containing the Payne Lesson Design.

APPENDIX B
Board of Health/Accountability

Improving Test Scores and Student Achievement: (page 94)

- Tracking student progress by quartile helps to measure student growth and determine the amount of probable progress in a given year. See form "Improving Test Scores and Student Achievement."

- Read the article by Ruby Payne titled "Campuswide Interventions That Improve Student Achievement" (pages 95-101).

APPENDIX C
Purpose/Structure/Patterns in Discipline

Purpose/Structure/Patterns in Disciplines (pages 104-113)

- Use the blank forms on page 104 to develop the structure of your discipline(s). Follow the many examples that are given in this appendix.

APPENDIX D
How to Use the Workbook Pages

Learning Structures: the *What*, the *Why*, the *How*

- Descriptions of all activities

APPENDIX E
Basic Concepts from *A Framework for Understanding Poverty* Workbook

- These pages are to be used as a review of Day One *A Framework for Understanding Poverty*. The appendix contains an article titled "*Understanding and Working with Adults and Students from Poverty*," along with charts on registers of language, resources, voices, and creating relationships.

BIBLIOGRAPHY

APPENDIX E
BASIC CONCEPTS FROM
A FRAMEWORK FOR UNDERSTANDING POVERTY WORKBOOK

Understanding and Working with Students and Adults from Poverty

By Ruby K. Payne, Ph.D.
Founder and President of aha! Process, Inc.

Although this article was originally written for teachers, the information presented may be of help to those who are working with persons making the transition from welfare to work.

To understand and work with students and adults from generational poverty, a framework is needed. This analytical framework is shaped around these basic ideas:

◆ Each individual has eight resources which greatly influence achievement; money is only one.

◆ Poverty is the extent to which an individual is without these eight resources.

◆ The hidden rules of the middle class govern schools and work; students from generational poverty come with a completely different set of hidden rules and do not know middle-class hidden rules.

◆ Language issues and the story structure of casual register cause many students from generational poverty to be unmediated, and therefore, the cognitive structures needed inside the mind to learn at the levels required by state tests have not been fully developed.

◆ Teaching is what happens outside the head; learning is what happens inside the head. For these students to learn, direct teaching must occur to build these cognitive structures.

◆ Relationships are the key motivators for learning for students from generational poverty.

Key points

Here are some key points that need to be addressed before discussing the framework:

Poverty is relative. If everyone around you has similar circumstances, the notion of poverty and wealth is vague. Poverty or wealth only exists in relationship to the known quantities or expectation.

Poverty occurs among people of all ethnic backgrounds and in all countries. The notion of a middle class as a large segment of society is a phenomenon of this century. The percentage of the population that is poor is subject to definition and circumstance.

Economic class is a continuous line, not a clear-cut distinction. Individuals move and are stationed all along the continuum of income.

Generational poverty and situational poverty are different. Generational poverty is defined as being in poverty for two generations or longer. Situational poverty exists for a shorter time is caused by circumstances like death, illness, or divorce.

This framework is based on patterns. All patterns have exceptions.

An individual bring with them the hidden rules of the class in which they were raised. Even though the income of the individual may rise significantly, many patterns of thought, social interaction, cognitive strategies, and so on remain with the individual.

School and businesses operate from middle-class norms and use the hidden rules of the middle class. These norms and hidden rules are never directly taught in schools or in businesses.

We must understand our students hidden rules and teach them the hidden middle-class rules that will make them successful at school and work. We can neither excuse them nor scold them for not knowing; we must teach them and provide support, insistence, and expectations.

To move from poverty to middle class or from middle class to wealth, an individual must give up relationships for achievement.

Resources

Poverty is defined as the "extent to which an individual does without resources. These are the resources that influence achievement:

Financial: the money to purchase goods and services.

Individuals who made it out of poverty usually cite an individual who made a significant difference for them.

Emotional: the ability to choose and control emotional responses, particularly to negative situations, without engaging in self-destructive behavior. This is an internal resource and shows itself through stamina, perseverance, and choices.

Mental: the necessary intellectual ability and acquired skills, such as reading, writing, and computing, to deal with everyday life.

Spiritual: a belief in divine purpose and guidance.

Physical: health and mobility.

Support systems: friends, family, backup resources and knowledge bases one can rely on in times of need. These are external resources.

Role models: frequent access to adults who are appropriate and nurturing to the child, and who do not engage in self-destructive behavior.

Knowledge of hidden rules: knowing the unspoken cues and habits of a group.

Language and story structure

To understand students and adults who come from a background of generational poverty, it's helpful be acquainted with the five registers of language. These are frozen, formal, consultative, casual, and intimate. Formal register is standard business and educational language. Formal register is characterized by complete sentences and specific word choice. Casual register is characterized by a 400- to 500-word vocabulary, broken sentences, and many non-verbal assists.

Maria Montano-Harmon, a California researcher, *has found that many low-income students know only casual register.* Many discipline referrals occur because the student has spoken in casual register. When individuals have no access to the structure and specificity of formal register, their achievement lags. This is complicated by the story structure used in casual register.

> ### The hidden rules of the middle class must be taught so students can choose to follow them if they wish.

In formal register, the story structure focuses on plot, has a beginning and end, and weaves sequence, cause and effect, characters, and consequences into the plot. In casual register, the focus of the story is characterization.

Typically, the story starts at the end (Joey busted his nose), proceeds with short vignettes interspersed with participatory comments from the audience (He hit him hard. BAM-BAM. You shouda' seen the blood on him), and finishes with a comment about the character. (To see this in action, watch a TV talk show where many of the participants use this structure.) The story elements that are included are those with emotional significance for the teller. This is an episodic, random approach with many omissions. It does not include sequence, cause and effect, or consequence.

Cognitive issues

The cognitive research indicates that early memory is linked to the predominant story structure that an individual knows. Furthermore, stories are retained in the mind longer than many other memory patterns for adults. Consequently, if a person has not had access to a story structure with cause and effect, consequence, and sequence, and lives in an environment where routine and structure are not available, he or she cannot plan.

According to Reuven Feuerstein, an Israeli educator:

◆ Individuals who cannot plan, cannot predict.

◆ If they cannot predict, they cannot identify cause and effect.

◆ If they cannot identify cause and effect, they cannot identify consequence.

◆ If they cannot identify consequence, they cannot control impulsivity.

◆ If they cannot control impulsivity, they have an inclination to criminal behavior.

Mediation

Feuerstein refers to these students as "unmediated." Simply explained mediation happens when an adult makes a deliberate intervention and does three things:

◆ points out the stimulus (what needs to be paid attention to)

◆ gives the stimulus meaning

◆ provides a strategy to deal with the stimulus.

For example: Don't cross the street without looking (stimulus). You could be killed (meaning). Look twice both ways before crossing (strategy).

Mediation builds cognitive strategies for the mind. The strategies are analogous to the infrastructure of house, that is, the plumbing, electrical and heating systems. When cognitive strategies are only partially in place, the mind can only partially accept the teaching. According to Feuerstein, unmediated students may miss as much as 50 percent of text on a page.

Why are so many students unmediated? Poverty forces one's time to be spent on survival. Many students from poverty live in single-parent families. When there is only one parent, he or she do not have time and energy to both mediate the children and work to put food on the table. And if the parent is nonmediated, his or her ability to mediate the children will be significantly lessened.

Hidden Class Rules

Generational Poverty	Middle Class	Wealth
The driving forces for decision-making are survival, relationships, and entertainment	The driving forces for decision-making are work and achievement.	The driving forces for decision-making are social, financial, and political connections.
People are possessions. It is worse to steal someone's girlfriend than a thing. A relationship is valued over achievement. That's why you must defend your child no matter what he or she has done. Too much education is feared because the individual might leave.	Things are possessions. If material security is threatened, often the relationship is broken.	Legacies, one-of-a-kind objects, and pedigrees are possessions.
The "world" is defined in local terms.	The "world" is defined in national terms.	The "world" is defined in international terms.
Physical fighting is how conflict is resolved. If you only know casual register, you don't have the words to negotiate a resolution. Respect is accorded to those who can physically defend themselves.	Fighting is done verbally. Physical fighting is viewed with distaste.	Fighting is done through social inclusion/exclusion and through lawyers.
Food is valued for its quantity.	Food is valued for its quality.	Food is valued for its presentation.

Other Rules

◆ You laugh when you are disciplined; it is a way to save face.

◆ The noise level is higher, nonverbal information is more important than verbal. Emotions are openly displayed, and the value of personality to the group is your ability to entertain.

◆ Destiny and fate govern. The notion of having choices is foreign. Discipline is about penance and forgiveness, not change.

◆ Tools are often not available. Therefore, the concepts of repair and fixing may not be present.

◆ Formal register is always used in an interview and is often an expected part of social interaction.

◆ Work is a daily part of life.

◆ Discipline is about changing behavior. To stay in the middle class, one must be self-governing and self-supporting.

◆ A reprimand is taken seriously (at least the pretense is there), without smiling and with some deference to authority.

◆ Choice is a key concept in the lifestyle. The future is very important. Formal education is seen as crucial for future success.

◆ The artistic and aesthetic are key to the lifestyle and included clothing, art, interior design, seasonal decorating, food, music, social activities, etc.

◆ For reasons of security and safety, virtually all contacts dependent on connection and introductions.

◆ Education is for the purpose of social, financial and political connections, as well as to enhance the artistic and aesthetic.

* One of the key differences between the well-to-do and the wealthy is that the wealthy almost always are patrons to the arts and often have an individual artist(s) to whom they are patrons as well.

To help students learn when they are only partially mediated, four structures must be built as part of direct teaching:

- ◆ the structure of the discipline,
- ◆ cognitive strategies,
- ◆ conceptual frameworks, and
- ◆ models for sorting out what is important from what is unimportant in text.

Hidden rules

One key resource for success in school and at work is an understanding of the hidden rules. Hidden rules are the unspoken cueing system that individuals use to indicate membership in a group. One of the most important middle-class rules is that work and achievement tend to be the driving forces in decision-making. In generational poverty, the driving forces are survival, entertainment, and relationships. This is why a student may have a $30 Halloween costume but an unpaid book bill.

Hidden rules shape what happens at school. For example, if the rule a students brings to school is to laugh when disciplined and he does so, the teacher is probably going to be offended. Yet for the student, this is the appropriate way to deal with the situation. The recommended approach is simply to teach the student that he needs a set of rules that brings success in school and at work and a different set that brings success outside of school. So, for example, if an employee laughs at a boss when being disciplined, he will probably be fired.

Many of the greatest frustrations teachers and administrators have with students from poverty is related to knowledge of the hidden rules. These students simply do not know middle-class hidden rules nor do most educators know the hidden rules of generational poverty.

To be successful, students must be given the opportunity to learn these rules. If they choose not to use them, that is their choice. But how can they make the choice if they don't know the rules exist?

Relationships are key

When individuals who made it out of poverty are interviewed, virtually all cite an individual who made a significant difference for them. Not only must the relationship be present, but tasks need to be referenced in terms of relationships.

For example, rather than talk about going to college, the conversation needs to be about how the learning will impact relationships. One teacher had this conversation with a 17-year-old student who didn't do his math homework on positive and negative numbers.

"Well," she said, "I guess it will be all right with you when your friends cheat you at cards. You won't know whether they're cheating you or not because you don't know positive and negative numbers, and they aren't going to let you keep score, either." He then used a deck of cards to show her that he know how to keep score. So she told him, "Then you know positive and negative numbers. I expect you to do your homework."

From that time on, he did his homework and kept an A average. The teacher simply couched the importance of the task according to the student's relationships.

Conclusion

Students from generational poverty need direct teaching to build cognitive structures necessary for learning. The relationships that will motivate them need to be established. The hidden rules must be taught so they can choose the appropriate responses if they desire.

Students from poverty are no less capable or intelligent. They simply have not been mediated in the strategies or hidden rules that contribute to success in school and at work.

References

Feuerstein, Reuven, et al. (1980), *Instrumental Enrichment: An Intervention Program for Cognitive Modifiability.* Glenview, IL: Scott, Foresman.

Joos, Martin. (1967) The Styles of the Five Clocks. *Language and Cultural Diversity in American Education,* 1972. Abrahams, R. D. and Troike, R. C., Eds. Englewood Cliffs, NJ: Prentice-Hall.

Making Schools Work for Children in Poverty: A New Framework Prepared by the Commission on Chapter 1, (1992). Washington, DC: AASA, December.

Montano-Harmon, Maria Rosario (1991). Discourse Features of Written Mexican Spanish: Current Research in Contrastive Rhetoric and Its Implications. *Hispania,* Vol. 74, No. 2, May 417-425.

Montano-Harmon, Maria Rosario (1994). Presentation given to Harris County Department of Education on the topic of her research findings.

Wheatley, Margaret J. (1992). *Leadership and the New Science.* San Francisco, CA: Berrett-Koehler Publishers.

Previously printed in *Instructional Leader* and *Focus* magazines.

Ruby K. Payne, Ph.D., founder and president of aha! Process, Inc. (1994), with more than 30 years experience as a professional educator, has been sharing her insights about the impact of poverty – and how to help educators and other professionals work effectively with individuals from poverty – in more than a thousand workshop settings through North America, Canada, and Australia.

More information on her book, *A Framework for Understanding Poverty,* can be found on her website, www.ahaprocess.com.

Registers of Language

REGISTER	EXPLANATION
FROZEN	Language that is always the same. For example: Lord's Prayer, wedding vows, etc.
FORMAL	The standard sentence syntax and word choice of work and school. Has complete sentences and specific word choice.
CONSULTATIVE	Formal register when used in conversation. Discourse pattern not quite as direct as formal register.
CASUAL	Language between friends and is characterized by a 400- to 800-word vocabulary. Word choice general and not specific. Conversation dependent upon non-verbal assists. Sentence syntax often incomplete.
INTIMATE	Language between lovers or twins. Language of sexual harassment.

Resources

FINANCIAL

Having the money to purchase goods and services.

EMOTIONAL

Being able to choose and control emotional responses, particularly to negative situations, without engaging in self-destructive behavior. This is an internal resource and shows itself through stamina, perseverance, and choices.

MENTAL

Having the mental abilities and acquired skills (reading, writing, computing) to deal with daily life.

SPIRITUAL

Believing in divine purpose and guidance.

PHYSICAL

Having physical health and mobility.

SUPPORT SYSTEMS

Having friends, family, and backup resources available to access in times of need. These are external resources.

RELATIONSHIPS/ROLE MODELS

Having frequent access to adult(s) who are appropriate, who are **nurturing** to the child, and who do not engage in self-destructive behavior.

KNOWLEDGE OF HIDDEN RULES

Knowing the unspoken cues and habits of a group.

Voices

CHILD

- Quit picking on me.
- You don't love me.
- You want me to leave.
- Nobody likes (loves) me.
- I hate you.
- You're ugly.
- You make me sick.
- It's your fault.
- Don't blame me.
- She, he, _____ did it.
- You make me mad.

PARENT

- You shouldn't (should) do that.
- It's wrong (right) to do …
- That's stupid, immature, out of line, ridiculous.
- Life's not fair. Get busy.
- You are good, bad, worthless, beautiful (any judgmental, evaluative comment).
- You do as I say.
- If you weren't so _____, this wouldn't happen to you.
- Why can't you be like _____?

ADULT

- In what ways could this be resolved?
- What factors will be used to determine the effectiveness, quality of …?
- I would like to recommend _____.
- What are choices in this situation?
- I am comfortable (uncomfortable) with _____.
- Options that could be considered are _____.
- For me to be comfortable, I need the following things to occur: _____.
- These are the consequences of that choice/action _____.
- We agree to disagree.

Adapted from work of Eric Berne

Creating Relationships

DEPOSITS	WITHDRAWALS
Seeking first to understand	Seeking first to be understood
Keeping promises	Breaking promises
Kindnesses, courtesies	Unkindnesses, discourtesies
Clarifying expectations	Violating expectations
Loyalty to the absent	Disloyalty, duplicity
Apologies	Pride, conceit, arrogance
Open to feedback	Rejecting feedback

Adapted from materials from The Seven Habits of Highly Effective People *by Stephen Covey*

DEPOSITS MADE TO INDIVIDUAL IN POVERTY	WITHDRAWALS MADE FROM INDIVIDUAL IN POVERTY
Appreciation for humor and entertainment provided by the individual	Put-downs or sarcasm about the humor or the individual
Acceptance of what the individual cannot say about a person or situation	Insistence and demands for full explanation about a person or situation
Respect for the demands and priorities of relationships	Insistence on the middle-class view of relationships
Using the adult voice	Using the parent voice
Assisting with goal-setting	Telling the individual his/her goals
Identifying options related to available resources	Making judgments on the value and availability of resources
Understanding the importance of personal freedom, speech, and individual personality	Assigning pejorative character traits to the individual

BIBLIOGRAPHY

Berliner, D.C. (1988). *Implications of Studies of Expertise in Pedagogy for Teacher Education and Evaluation*. Paper presented at 1988 Educational Testing Service Invitational Conference on New Directions for Teacher Assessment. New York, NY.

Begley, Sharon. (2003). Diet during pregnancy could have effects that last to adulthood. Science Journal column in *Wall Street Journal* (Midwest Edition). New York, NY: Dow Jones & Co.

Berne, Eric (1996). *Games People Play: The Basic Handbook of Transactional Analysis*. New York, NY: Ballantine Books.

Bloom, Benjamin. (1976). *Human Characteristics and School Learning*. New York, NY: McGraw-Hill Book Company.

Caine, Renate Nummela, & Caine, Geoffrey. (1991). *Making Connections: Teaching and the Human Brain*. Alexandria, VA: Association of Supervision & Curriculum Development.

Collins, Bryn C. (1997). *Emotional Unavailability: Recognizing It, Understanding It, and Avoiding Its Trap*. Lincolnwood, IL: NTC/Contemporary Publishing Company.

Covey, Stephen R. (1989). *The Seven Habits of Highly Effective People: Powerful Lessons in Personal Change*. New York, NY: Simon & Schuster.

Feuerstein, Reuven, et al. (1980). *Instrumental Enrichment: An Intervention Program for Cognitive Modifiability*. Glenview, IL: Scott, Foresman & Co.

Idol, Lorna, & Jones, B.F. (Eds.). (1991). *Educational Values and Cognitive Instruction: Implications for Reform*. Hillsdale, NJ: Lawrence Erlbaum Associates.

Jones, B.F., Pierce, J., & Hunter, B. (1988). Teaching students to construct graphic representations. *Educational Leadership*. Volume 46 (4), 20-25.

Jones, Raymond C. *Vocabulary Word Map*. www.readingquest.org.,

Marzano, Robert J., & Arredondo, Daisy. (1986). *Tactics for Thinking*. Aurora, CO: Mid Continent Regional Educational Laboratory.

Palincsar, Annemarie S., & Brown, A.L. (1984). The reciprocal teaching of comprehension-fostering and comprehension-monitoring activities. *Cognition and Instruction*. Volume 1 (2), 117-175.

Payne, Ruby K. (2002). *Understanding Learning: the How, the Why, the What*. Highlands, TX: **aha!** Process

Payne, Ruby K. (2003). *A Framework for Understanding Poverty* (Third Revised Edition). Highlands, TX: **aha!** Process

Sharron, Howard, & Coulter, Martha. (1994). *Changing Children's Minds: Feuerstein's Revolution in the Teaching of Intelligence.* Exeter, Great Britain: BPC Wheatons Ltd.

Wolin, Steven J., & Wolin, Sybil. (1994). *The Resilient Self: How Survivors of Troubled Families Rise Above Adversity.* New York, NY: Villard Books.

District 220 Teachers, Barrington, Illinois, used the following resources:

Carr, Eileen, & Wilson, Karen K.. (1986). Guidelines for evaluating vocabulary instruction. *Journal of Reading.* Volume 29 (7).

Graves, Michael F., & Prenn, Maureen C. (1986). Costs and benefits of various methods of teaching vocabulary. *Journal of Reading.* Volume 29 (7).

Stahl, Steven A. (1990). Beyond the instrumentalist hypothesis: some relationships between word meanings and comprehension. Champaign-Urbana, IL: University of Illinois at Champaign-Urbana.

Stahl, Steven A. (1986). Principles of Effective Vocabulary Instruction. *Journal of Reading.* Volume 29 (7).

Eye-openers at ...

Interested in more information?

We invite you to our website, www.ahaprocess.com to join our **aha!** News List!

Receive the latest income and poverty statistics free when you join! Then receive **aha!** News, and periodic updates!

Also on the website:

- Success stories from our participants—from schools, social services, and businesses
- Three new workshops!
- Four Trainer Certification programs
- An up-to-date listing of our books & videos
- A convenient online store
- Dr. Ruby Payne's U.S. National Tour dates
- A videoclip of Dr. Payne
- News articles from around the country

And more at ...

www.ahaprocess.com

www.ahaprocess.com
PO Box 727, Highlands, TX 77562-0727
(800) 424-9484; fax: (281) 426-8705
store@ahaprocess.com

ORDER FORM

UPS SHIP TO ADDRESS: (no post office boxes, please)

NAME: _____ E-mail _____

ORGANIZATION: _____

ADDRESS: _____

CITY/STATE/ZIP: _____

TELEPHONE: _____ FAX: _____

QTY	TITLE	1-4 Copies	5+ Copies*	Total
	A Framework for Understanding Poverty	22.00	15.00	
	A Framework for Understanding Poverty Workbook	7.00	7.00	
	Understanding Learning (for Day 2 training order set below)	7.00	7.00	
	Learning Structures Workbook *(for Day 2 training, order set below)*	7.00	7.00	
	Understanding Learning/Learning Structures workbook (bundled set for Day 2)	10.00	10.00	
	A Framework for Understanding Poverty Audio Workshop Kit (includes Day 1 & 2 8 CDs –and 4 books listed above) **S/H: $10.50**	225.00	225.00	
	Un Marco Para Entender La Pobreza	22.00	15.00	
	A Framework for Understanding Poverty Audio CD Set/Book	35.00	35.00	
	Putting the Pieces Together workbook (replaces Application of Learning Structures)	10.00	10.00	
	A Picture Is Worth a Thousand Words	18.00	15.00	
	Berrytales – Plays in One Act	25.00	20.00	
	Bridges Out of Poverty: Strategies for Professionals & Communities	22.00	15.00	
	Changing Children's Minds	30.00	30.00	
	Crossing the Tracks for Love	14.95	14.95	
	Daily Math Practice for Virginia SOLs – Grade 4	22.00	15.00	
	Daily Math Skills Review Grade 4- practice for mastery of math standards	22.00	15.00	
	Getting Ahead in a Just Gettin'-By World & Facilitator Notes (set)	25.00	25.00	
	Getting Ahead in a Just Gettin'-By World (after purchasing a set)	15.00	15.00	
	Getting Ahead in a Just Gettin'-By World Facilitator Notes (after set)	10.00	10.00	
	Hear Our Cry: Boys in Crisis	22.00	15.00	
	Hidden Rules of Class at Work	22.00	15.00	
	Living on a Tightrope: a Survival Handbook for Principals	22.00	15.00	
	Mr. Base Ten Invents Mathematics	22.00	15.00	
	Parenting Someone Else's Child: The Foster Parents' How-To Manual	22.00	15.00	
	Removing the Mask: Giftedness in Poverty	25.00	20.00	
	Environmental Opportunity Profile (25/set-incl 1 FAQ)	25.00	25.00	
	Addit'l FAQs Environmental Opportunities Profile manual	3.00	3.00	
	Slocumb-Payne Teacher Perception Inventory (25/set)	25.00	25.00	
	Think Rather of Zebra	18.00	15.00	
	Trainer's Companion: Stories to Stimulate Reflection, Conversation, Action	22.00	15.00	
	What Every Church Member Should Know About Poverty	22.00	15.00	
	Tucker Signing Strategies Video & Manual **S/H: $8.50**	195.00	195.00	
	Tucker Signs Reference Cards on CD	25.00	25.00	
	Take-Home Books for Tucker Signing Strategies for Reading	22.00	15.00	
	Preventing School Violence – 5 videos & manual **S/H: $15.00**	995.00	995.00	
	Preventing School Violence CD – PowerPoint presentation	25.00	25.00	
	Preventing School Violence Training Manual	15.00	15.00	
	Audiotapes, What Every Church Member Should Know About Poverty	25.00	25.00	
	Meeting Standards & Raising Test Scores When You Don't Have Much Time or Money (4 videos/training manual **S/H: $15.00**	995.00	995.00	
	Meeting Standards & Raising Test Scores Training Manual	18.00	18.00	
	Meeting Standards & Raising Test Scores Resource Manual	18.00	18.00	
	Meeting Standards & Raising Test Scores CD – PowerPoint presentation	50.00	50.00	
	Rita's Stories (2 videos) **S/H: $8.50** Rita's Stories DVD **S/H: $4.50**	150.00	150.00	
	Ruby Payne Video or DVD Sampler **S/H: $4.50**	10.00	10.00	
	aha! 12 oz. mugs (white with red logo and website)	8.00	2@15.00	
	Rubygems! 16-month Planner – Educator/Parent Relationships	10.00	10+ 8.00	
	Walk-through Rubric Notepads – *Circle one:* General; Mutual Respect; Instruction; Discipline & Classroom Management, Audit for Differentiated Instruction, Assorted	5@5.00	50@30.00	

For Certified Trainers Only – Please note date/city of training:

		1-4	5+	Total
	A Framework for Understanding Poverty Video Sets (12 modules) (Day 1 & Day 2 of Framework seminar) Circle one: VHS or DVD **S/H: $25.00**	1995.00	1995.00	
	A Framework for Understanding Poverty CD – PowerPoint presentation	50.00	50.00	
	A Framework for Understanding Poverty CD – Enhanced PowerPoint pres.	100.00	100.00	
	Bridges Out of Poverty CD – PowerPoint presentation	50.00	50.00	

Total Quantity	
Subtotal	
S/H	
Tax	
Total	

TERMS: S/H: 1-4 books – $4.50 plus $2.00 each additional book up to 4 books, [1 calendar $2]
   5+ books – 8% of total, *(special S/H for videos).* E-mail for international rates.
TAX: 6.25% Texas residents only   Prices subject to change. Visit website for current offerings.

AmEx   MC   Visa   Discover

CREDIT CARD # _____ EXP. DATE _____ Signature _____

AUTHORIZATION # _____ PO # _____ (please fax PO with order) Check # _____.

*Orders placed by participants while attending U.S. National Tour or Trainer Certification are given quantity (5 or more) pricing.